P. sepngnano

Campus floreus

P. scu spcus

Ludneroγ

Sca cohanis

hospital
scs

scs

sca petri

P. potr
firis

Sblasi

cesari
tumul

Mole adriane q̃ & P. collina
et

Bernide sepul
et

P. uridaria q̃
& sci petri

Houa Turris

MICHELANGELO

THE SISTINE CHAPEL CEILING, ROME

Loren Partridge

GEORGE BRAZILLER   NEW YORK

ACKNOWLEDGMENTS

I thank Leslie Martin and Wendy Partridge for reading the manuscript and for many valuable suggestions. Special thanks to the publisher, George Braziller, who supported this project, even after a two-year delay, and to Adrienne Baxter, for her good sense and fine editorial skills.

First published in 1996 by George Braziller, Inc.
Text copyright © 1996 by George Braziller, Inc.
Color illustrations by Takashi Okamura © NTV, Tokyo.

For information, please address the publisher:
George Braziller, Inc.
171 Madison Avenue
New York, New York 10016

Library of Congress Cataloging-in-Publication Data:
Partridge, Loren W.
    Michelangelo : The Sistine Chapel ceiling, Rome / Loren Partridge.
    p.   cm.
    Includes bibliographical references.
    ISBN 0-8076-1315-0
    1. Mural painting and decoration, Italian—Vatican City. 2. Mural painting and decoration, Renaissance—Vatican City. 3. Ceilings—Vatican City. 4. Michelangelo Buonarroti, 1475-1564—Criticism and interpretation. 5. Sistine Chapel (Vatican Palace, Vatican City) I. Title
ND2757.V35P37 1996   96-31543
759.5—dc20   CIP

Page 1: Pietro del Massaio's plan of Rome, Biblioteca Apostolica Vaticana, Vatican City
Frontispiece: Michelangelo, The *Erythraean Sibyl* (detail), The Sistine Chapel ceiling (see pl. 25, page 84)

Printed by G. Canale & C., Arese, Italy

CONTENTS

In memory of Rosemary

PREFACE

The Sistine Chapel ceiling frescoes of 1508–12 by Michelangelo Buonarroti (1475–1564) remain one of the greatest masterpieces of western art (Plate 1, fig. 1). In this book the ceiling frescoes are discussed within the context of their site, cultural circumstances, production, narrative and compositional structure, style, and theological significance. I have benefited greatly from the many recent studies cited in the notes and bibliography. Few, however, treat these frescoes comprehensively or do justice to their multilayered complexity. It is a fundamental premise of this essay that these frescoes, like all great works of art, simultaneously communicate many overlapping, often conflicting messages. The reader, therefore, should be prepared to juggle mentally many themes at once.

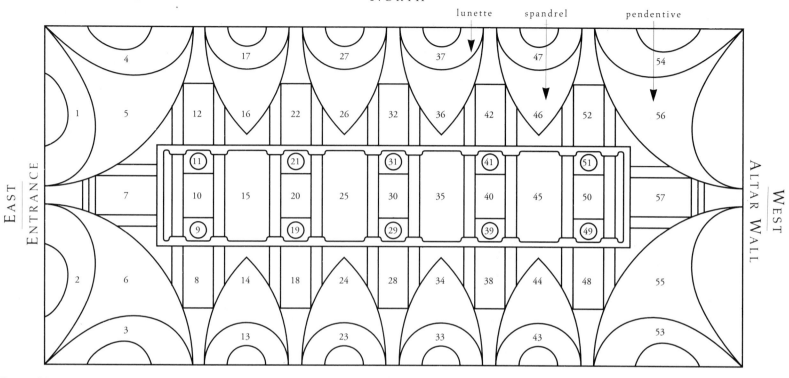

NORTH

lunette · spandrel · pendentive

EAST · ENTRANCE

WEST · ALTAR WALL

CENTRAL NARRATIVES
10. The Drunkenness of Noah
15. The Flood
20. The Sacrifice of Noah
25. Temptation and Expulsion
30. The Creation of Eve
35. The Creation of Adam
40. The Separation of Water from
    Firmament and Water Brings
    Forth Life
45. The Creation of Sun, Moon,
    and Plants
50. The Separation of Light and Dark

PENDENTIVES
5. Judith and Holofernes
6. David and Goliath
55. The Death of Haman
56. The Brazen Serpent

PROPHETS AND SIBYLS
7. Zechariah
8. Joel
12. Delphic Sibyl
18. Erythræan Sibyl
22. Isaiah
28. Ezekiel

32. Cumæan Sibyl
38. Persian Sibyl
42. Daniel
48. Jeremiah
52. Libyan Sibyl
57. Jonah

MEDALLIONS
9. Antiochus Epiphanes Falls from
   His Chariot
11. Death of Razis
19. Mattathias Pulls Down the
    Altar in Modein

21. Expulsion of Heliodorus
29. Death of Nicanor
31. Alexander the Great before the
    High Priest of Jerusalem
39. Elisha Cures Naaman of
    Leprosy[?]
41. Death of Absalom
49. Ascension of Elijah
51. Abraham's Sacrifice of Isaac

ANCESTORS OF CHRIST
1. Eleazar-Matthan
2. Jacob-Joseph

3. Achim-Eliud
4. Azor-Sadoch
13-14. Zorobabel-Abiud-Eliachim
16-17. Josias-Jechonias-Salathiel
23-24. Ozias-Joatham-Achaz
26-27. Ezechias-Manasses-Amon
33-34. Roboam-Abias
36-37. Asa-Josaphat-Joram
43-44. Salmon-Boaz-Obed
46-47. Jesse-David-Solomon
53. Aminadab
54. Naason

Fig. 1 - Diagram of the Sistine Chapel ceiling

INTRODUCTION

Fig. 2 - Reconstruction of the exterior of the Sistine Chapel

THE SISTINE CHAPEL BEFORE MICHELANGELO

*T*he Sistine Chapel, built between 1477 and 1481, takes its name from its patron, Pope Sixtus IV (papacy 1471–84).[1] The architect of the chapel, Baccio Pontelli (c. 1450–92), incorporated into his project the foundations and walls of an earlier chapel, which was first documented in 1368 and probably had a wooden ceiling. The new chapel's exterior is fortified with massive sloping walls and battlements (fig. 2). A slightly flattened barrel vault spans its vast interior (figs. 3–4). The proportions of the chapel—roughly 1:3 and 1:2 [approx. 133 x 46 x 62 feet (approx. 40.5 x 14 x 19 m)]—echo those of Solomon's Temple of Jerusalem described in the Old Testament (1 Kings 6:2). Between 1481 and 1483 the walls were decorated with frescoes by Pietro Perugino (c. 1450–1523), Pinturicchio (c. 1454–1513), Domenico Ghirlandaio (1449–94), Sandro Botticelli (1445–1510), Luca Signorelli (1445/50–1523), and Cosimo Rosselli (1439–1507).

The lowest of three levels was decorated by imitation tapestries. Perugino's painting of the *Assumption and Coronation of the Virgin* stood above the altar on the west wall. Its subject referred directly to the chapel's dedication on 15 August 1483 to the Assumption of the Virgin. The middle zone was frescoed with scenes from the life

Fig. 3 - Reconstruction of the interior of the Sistine Chapel in the fifteenth century, looking west toward the altar

Fig. 4 - Interior of the Sistine Chapel, looking east toward the entrance

of Moses on the left and the life of Christ on the right. The two cycles began on either side of the altar, unfolded chronologically in two parallel bands down the long south and north walls, and terminated on the east entrance wall. In the upper band the first thirty-two popes were painted within illusionistic niches. The series likewise began on the altar wall, but then progressed chronologically zigzag from one side of the chapel to the other before ending on the entrance wall.[2] Not only did the subject matter and organization of the fifteenth-century decoration strongly influence Michelangelo's ceiling design, as we shall see, so too did the series of triumphal arches suggested by the pairs of illusionistic niches flanking the windows.

It is unknown whether or not the lunettes and spandrels were decorated, but the barrel vault was probably painted about 1479–80 following a design by Pier Matteo d'Amelia (active 1467–1503/8) (fig. 5). Drawing on a tradition going back to antiquity, which associated ceilings with heaven, the design illusionistically painted away the vault to reveal a deep blue sky with gilt stars and the zodiacal band. Michelangelo's design, as is discussed later in this essay, also relates to this tradition.

THE CHAPEL'S FUNCTION[3]

The scale, strength, and splendor of the Sistine Chapel were intended to heighten the majesty and authority of a corporate body known as the *capella papalis*, or Papal Chapel. It was composed of the pope and about two hundred high-ranking ecclesiastical and secular officials who were required to meet at least forty-two times a year and participate in at least twenty-seven Masses. With ceremonies often running several hours, this educated and elite group had more than sufficient time to contemplate the full range of possible meanings of the Michelangelo's ceiling decoration.

A marble *cancellata*, or screen, divided the chapel in half (figs. 4, 6), a fact of considerable importance for understanding Michelangelo's ceiling. The eastern half was occupied by lay and clerical observers who were not members of the Papal Chapel. The western half—one step higher, called the *sancta sanctorum*—was reserved for the *capella papalis*. The top of the *cancellata* featured seven candelabra that imitated those from the Constantinian Church of Santa Costanza in Rome. The screen was moved eastward to its present location about 16 feet 5 inches (5 meters) closer to the entrance in the mid-sixteenth century to accommodate an ever-growing papal court. At that time an eighth candlestick was added in place of the cantoria, or singing gallery. Paris de Grassis (1470–1528), the Master of Ceremonies for Pope Julius II (papacy 1503–13), recorded that the candelabra symbolized an imperial-like processional prerogative of the pope dating back to a gift in the early fourth century A.D. from Emperor Constantine (ruled A.D. 306–37), who first united the church and the Roman Empire. They also recalled the menorah of the Temple of Jerusalem (Exodus 37:17–24), the seven gifts of the Holy Spirit (Isaiah 11:2–3), and the seven candles of the apocalypse that signified the seven churches of Asia Minor (Revelation 2:1). These associations not only represented the church's claim to universal temporal and spiritual sovereignty but also suggested that the papal chapel was a new Temple of Jerusalem suffused with the Holy Spirit and the center of

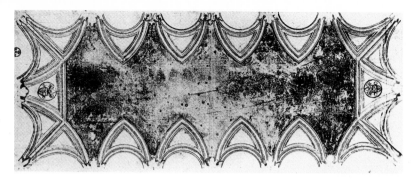

Fig. 5 - Pier Matteo d'Amelia, *Design for the Sistine Chapel Ceiling*, Florence, Uffizi

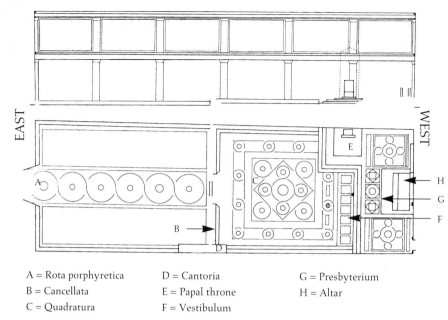

A = Rota porphyretica   D = Cantoria   G = Presbyterium
B = Cancellata   E = Papal throne   H = Altar
C = Quadratura   F = Vestibulum

Fig. 6 - Plan and lower elevation of the Sistine Chapel in the 15th and early 16th centuries

the New Dispensation in the West supplanting the Old Dispensation in the East.

The chapel's pavement pattern of six interlocked circles marked the processional route the pope and his entourage followed when entering the *sancta sanctorum* through the eastern half of the chapel between two rows of Swiss guards. It also indicated the ceremonial route taken by the pope during the Mass when he exited from the chapel to collect the reserved Host from the Chapel of S. Nicholas across the adjoining Sala Regia. Upon returning, he knelt with the Host on the large porphyry disk adorning the first circle, which imitated a similarly placed *rota porphyretica* in St. Peter's. In assessing Michelangelo's ceiling, it is important to note that from here the pope could take in the entire chapel with one commanding glance. In addition, the porphyry disk and the Cosmatesque floor, like the candelabra, were understood to be Constantinian revivals, signs that the pope was heir to Constantine's imperial authority.

The large square in the pavement of the *sancta sanctorum* defined an area called the *quadratura*. Tapestry-covered wooden benches for the cardinals were arranged around it on three sides. The rest of the Papal Chapel sat in designated places according to rank on the marble benches, the steps, and the floor surrounding and within the *quadratura*. The design of rectangles between the *quadratura* and the steps demarcated the vestibulum across which the pope moved in a procession to his canopy-covered throne raised on a podium and a dais to the left of the altar. Reached by three steps—a fourth was added in the mid-sixteenth century to provide more seating—the podium was an extension of the presbyterium or presbytery. The altar, placed in the center of the presbytery, was the ritual focus of the chapel. Michelangelo's ceiling decoration, not surprisingly, thus both begins and culminates above the altar.

MICHELANGELO'S COMMISSION[4]

The Sistine Chapel stands on one of the Vatican's lowest sites. Drainage problems soon weakened the foundations, causing the south wall to lean outward. In the spring of 1504, a large crack appeared in the northwest corner of the vault to the right of the altar. Its rapid progression down the center of the vault forced the closure of the chapel. By 18 October 1504, the structure had been stabilized by the installation of iron rods below the chapel floor and through the crown of the vault. These rods tied together the opposing north and south walls, although the problem was not definitively solved until three external buttresses were built between 1566 and 1568 by Pirro Ligorio (c. 1510–83) and Nanni di Baccio Bigio (d. 1568). In view of the vault's disfigurement by the crack and the installation of the tie rods, Pope Julius II commissioned Michelangelo to fresco the ceiling sometime between 1504 and 1506 for 3,000 ducats, a princely sum. Work began about 10 May 1508 when Michelangelo recorded his first payment. In a letter of 1523, Michelangelo stated that he had originally been commissioned to paint the Twelve Apostles but, believing that it "would turn out a poor thing," was given permission "to do what I liked."

SACRED ORATORY[5]

Whether or not Michelangelo did as he liked or was advised by the pope and his theologians is unknown and much debated. But it is clear that the general content of the ceiling is closely related to the sacred oratory that Julius II heard preached in the Sistine Chapel throughout his forty-two-year career first as cardinal and then as pope. Based on the revival of classical epideictic rhetoric, the rhetoric of praise and blame, sermons delivered in the chapel were intended less to present new ideas than to celebrate traditional ones. Praise of God's creation and especially praise of Christ's Incarnation—understood as the cosmic center of all space and time, the event that restored and made whole the universe after the Fall of humankind—were principal themes of these sermons and of the Sistine ceiling.

As a style of discourse, sacred oratory often appealed to the sense of sight, with auditors regularly asked to visualize scenes outside of themselves. This practice encouraged sumptuous artistic commissions such as the Sistine ceiling, even if it would soon be challenged by iconoclastic reformers. Sacred oratory also imitated ancient models, yet simultaneously attempted to surpass them by using individual judgment and reference to present circumstances. Similarly, emulation of antiquity and a self-conscious striving for exceptional originality, which aimed to outdo both nature and other Renaissance masters, characterized Michelangelo's High Renaissance style in the ceiling.

THE PATRON[6]

Imitation and innovation were also the hallmarks of the Julian regime. Julius II (fig. 7) pursued political, religious, and artistic policies nearly identical to those of Sixtus IV, who had established his nephew's career when he made him a cardinal in 1471. Julius II (Giuliano della Rovere) executed these policies, however, with much greater scope, dynamism, and aggressiveness than had his uncle Sixtus IV (Francesco della Rovere). His commission for the decoration of the Sistine ceiling, for example, was a typical extension of an earlier Sistine project, but characteristically far grander, offering an unrivaled opportunity to Michelangelo.

Again, following the lead of Sixtus IV, but with far more vigor, Julius II devoted most of his considerable energy to strengthening papal control over Rome and Italy in the face of increasing defections from the church and decreasing financial resources. Donning armor, personally leading his troops, recapturing Bologna from the upstart Bentivogli family, driving the "barbarian" French from Italy, Julius expanded the Papal States to their farthest limits ever and consolidated papal power for the church's political and economic survival. No wonder, then, that more than half the scenes on the fictive bronze medallions in the Sistine ceiling were chosen from the religious wars chronicled in Maccabees and that the triumphal conclusion of book two—the killing of Nicanor, the great enemy of God's chosen people, by the warrior-priest, Judas Maccabeus—was featured at the center.

In 1505, Julius boldly ordered the destruction of the old Constantinian basilica of St. Peter's, one of the largest and most revered churches in Christendom, and began its rebuilding according to the

Fig. 7 - Raphael, *Portrait of Pope Julius II,* London, National Gallery, 1511-12

plan of Donato Bramante (1444–1514) for a gigantic centrally planned martyrium inspired by the Pantheon and the basilica of Constantine, the so-called Temple of Peace. The proportions, geometry, and classical references of New St. Peter's were understood by contemporaries as potent symbols of church renewal and papal power. Placement of the great dome over the tomb of St. Peter confirmed that papal primacy derived directly from Christ by way of St. Peter, since Christ had made Peter—and, according to the doctrine of the Petrine Succession, his successors as well—his vicar on earth with the power of "the keys to the kingdom of heaven" to save and to damn (Matthew 16:18–19). Ironically, Julius II's grant of indulgences to help pay for New St. Peter's was one of the immediate causes of the Protestant Reformation, the most serious threat to papal authority in its entire history. Precisely this kind of resistance to the papacy prompted allusions in the medallions of the Sistine ceiling to the power of the keys and to the rebuilding and renewing of the church in the person of Ezekiel located at the ceiling's center. Further, the Renaissance development of an increasingly princely and dynastic papacy to strengthen church leadership is reflected in the ceiling by the profusion of decorative swags composed of acorns and oaks, personal emblems of the della Rovere family. Finally, the crescendo of challenges to Julius's power in the course of his regime may well be mirrored by the increasing dynamism, urgency, and even (in the pendentives) violence of Michelangelo's art as he proceeded from one campaign of frescoes to the next.

One of the greatest threats to the Julian regime was the schismatic Council of Pisa. Called in 1511 by King Louis XII of France (1462–1515), who was supported by the French cardinals, it set out to depose the pope. Julius was forced to counter with the convocation of the Fifth Lateran Council (1512–17), which began the difficult process of addressing critical and long-delayed issues of church reform. In July 1512, the council affirmed in dogmatic decrees the doctrine of individual immortality, which proclaimed personal rather than collective integrity in eternity as well as in history. This doctrine provided a context for the colossal egos of both the patron and the artist, each of whom would have viewed his own deeds—deliberate attempts to change the course of church or artistic history—as heroic self-sacrifices offered as meritorious works in the cause of his own salvation. The doctrine also supported the ceiling's insistence on individual responsibility in the process of salvation. It had always been believed, however, that individual will had to be channeled through the church. And in triumph or defeat, Julius consistently turned to his personal protectress, the Virgin Mary, embodiment of the church. The *Creation of Eve* in the center of the Sistine ceiling is just one of many manifestations of Julius's special devotion to the Virgin, who was prefigured by Eve.

Julius followed an imperial model whether playing the role of patron, prince, or priest in his attempt to restore what he believed to be the lofty destiny of the Roman Church. By his papal name, he assumed the warriorlike persona of Julius Caesar (100–44 B.C.). When he recited passages from Virgil's *Aeneid* to spur his troops in the campaign to recover Bologna or when he commissioned a Virgilian *Juliad* from Marco Girolamo Vida (1480/85–1566) to recount his deeds, Julius emulated the first Roman emperor, Augustus (ruled 27 B.C.—A.D. 14). And when he had built in front of St. Peter's a replica of the Arch of Constantine decorated with scenes of the conquest of Bologna as the culminating prop of his victorious entry into Rome on Palm Sunday, 28 March 1507, he was both reenacting Christ's entry into Jerusalem and renewing Constantine's divinely inspired victory over Maxentius, which, it was believed, had led to Constantine's conversion to Christianity and to his Edict of Milan, which granted freedom of religion to Christians in the Roman Empire, and to his active state support for Christianity. With a typically Julian touch, Giles of Viterbo (1469–1532), general of the Augustinian order and unofficial spokesman for the Julian Age, claimed that Julius II far surpassed any emperor because papal authority now extended to the New World, unknown in antiquity.

Images in the Sistine ceiling further construct Julius's imperial persona. The Cumæan Sibyl and the medallion with Alexander the Great above her, again significantly located at the center of the ceiling, allude, as we shall see, to Julius II's fulfillment of the destiny of Augustus's Julian line and to his possession of a sovereignty more immense than that even of Alexander. The wide geographical distribution of the sibyls may refer to the imperial dominion of the church. And by the use of motifs from the Arch of Constantine in the general layout of the ceiling, Michelangelo recalls Constantine and his imperial authority, which, it was believed, the emperor had bequeathed to the popes.

This imperialism was closely related to a long European tradition of prophetic millennialism, particularly vital in the early-sixteenth-century writings of Giles of Viterbo. Popular theory held that the millennium and the Second Coming of Christ, which would bring history to a close, were to be announced both by a time of troubles and by a period of religious, political, intellectual, and artistic renewal. Signs of troubles and renewal could be seen everywhere, and the growth of the imperium—the conquest of the New World and the reconquest and expansion of the Papal States—pointed to the coming of millennial peace when the world would be unified, pacified, and Christianized. When in 1506 Giles of Viterbo preached to the *capella papalis* that the liberation of the Papal States was but a prelude to Julius II's plan for a crusade to recover Constantinople and Jerusalem from the Turks, a necessary final stage before the millennium, he gave voice to the Julian Age's strong sense of imminence and culmination—of being at both the cutting edge and the transcendent end of history—with Rome and the Vatican at the sacred center of the universe, soon to become the eternal seat of a new golden age. The paradoxes of the church's simultaneously suffering attack and leading renewal, embracing all time and ending time, are important millennial themes of the ceiling, as we shall see.

In this climate of millennial expectation, Julius II developed a correspondingly apocalyptic personality that enabled him to overcome nearly insuperable obstacles through the force of a temperament described by contemporaries as "violent," "audacious," "unstable," "hasty," "rash," and "choleric." He often manifested a brute animal force and primitive rage perceived to be akin to divine power, making all tremble before his volcanic fulminations. In 1512, Giles of Viterbo even compared Julius's deeds to God's creation. Cristoforo Marcello (active c. 1500–27), in a speech the same year before the Fifth Lateran Council, called the pope "another God on earth." And in a treatise on the Eucharist dedicated to Julius II, Cipriano Benet (d. 1522), Dominican doctor of theology and professor at the University of Rome, equated the mystical body of Christ in the Mass with the presence of divinity in the pope. A deinotic personality, summed up by the Italian word *terribilità*, also characterized Michelangelo, whom Julius treated as an equal, even thrashing with his terrible stick a monsignor who once dared to say against Michelangelo that artists were "ignorant of everything except their art." The power and grandeur of God's creative acts represented in the Sistine ceiling, as well as the superhuman concentration and energy needed for their conception and execution, mirror the *terribilità* of both the patron and the artist as well as the period's sense of millennial renewal.

Said to suffer from gout, syphilis, and bouts of drunkenness, Julius II was thought more than once to be at death's door, only to rebound again with full energy. But delicate health and serious threats to his regime produced episodes of dark brooding and depression, a trait shared with the saturnine Michelangelo, as his letters and poetry reveal. The brooding of some of the prophets and sibyls, especially Jeremiah, painted by Michelangelo and the sense of helplessness in the face of impending doom and death implicit in much of the decoration, discussed later in this essay, resonate with these aspects of the character of both Julius and Michelangelo as well as with the gloomy underside of millennialism.

THE ARTIST[7]

Renaissance artists, the majority of whom came from lower-class backgrounds, learned their trades through an apprenticeship system tightly controlled by one of several guilds, depending on the medium. Since artists worked with their hands for pay, they were considered to be artisans, practitioners of the mechanical arts, and of low social status—much below that of merchants, bankers, nobles, and the university-educated elite trained in the liberal arts. Exceptionally, Michelangelo's father, who owned land and held minor governmental positions, lived the life of an impoverished gentleman and, according to the artist and art historian Giorgio Vasari (1511–74), believed that his son disgraced the Buonarroti family by becoming an artist. The story may be a myth but, even so, still indicates the low regard in which artists could be held.

Michelangelo's activity as an artist, however, coincided with the development of a classically derived theory, first revived in the Renaissance by architect, painter, and author Leon Battista Alberti (1406–72), that placed art among the liberal arts. This was so, the theory held, because artists needed considerable knowledge of such things as geometry, mathematics, and classical culture. In addition, they had the godlike ability to reproduce nature, to create newly imagined and even fantastic worlds, and to suggest divine perfection in transcendent images of surpassing beauty. This rise in the status of artists was a product of the Italian courts, because artists could also present their princely patrons, such as Julius II, in images that reinforced their claims to dominion and divine favor. The courts also gave birth to the art academy, which promoted the intellectual and creative side of art and claimed that artists were gentlemen and, at their best, semidivinities. The academy also unified all art production directly under state control, thereby transforming artists from guildsmen into courtiers. This atmosphere led contemporaries to call Michelangelo "divine" and Michelangelo himself to claim (falsely) that he had not trained as an apprentice and had never maintained a *bottega*, or workshop.

While no Renaissance artist received the university education required for a true practitioner of the liberal arts, the heady atmosphere of the courts produced artists with literary aspirations, such as

Michelangelo, who wrote poetry of considerable distinction throughout his life. It also led many to aspire to noble titles, wealth, and status. Michelangelo, for example, claimed (again falsely) descent from the counts of Canossa, commanded high prices for his works, and rejected obligations if not treated with respect. Although he was widely sought after by the ruling and educated elite of Rome and Florence, hurtful slights, irregular payments, and humiliating subservience were also part of his reality.

The new emphasis on intellectual creativity rather than manual dexterity prompted the most ambitious artists to strive to advance art by innovation, to develop unique individual styles, to exceed their own previous best efforts and those of rival artists for the greater glory of themselves, their patrons, and God. Art was thus perceived as an evolutionary process constantly reaching new heights; Vasari wrote in his 1550 edition of *Lives of the Most Eminent Painters, Sculptors, and Architects* that art had evolved through three ages culminating in Michelangelo at a final age of perfection.

Such were the circumstances of Michelangelo's execution of the Sistine ceiling frescoes. They help to explain the artist's intense rivalry with Bramante and Raphael and his almost superhuman physical energy, his extraordinary stylistic evolution and awesome creative power—a force beyond anything he or his rivals had ever previously generated. The impact of his virtuoso demonstration in the Sistine Chapel was huge and immediate, virtually changing the course of art history. The ceiling provided an unprecedented model of heroicized papal ideals and aspirations, all the while holding the conflicts and contradictions of the Julian Age within a High Renaissance equilibrium. It also contained all the elements that would produce a fundamental stylistic shift from a High Renaissance to a Mannerist style provoked by the deepening cultural crises of the following decades.

SCAFFOLDS, CAMPAIGNS, AND TECHNIQUES[8]

Michelangelo devised a suspended bridgelike scaffold to allow the chapel to be used throughout the course of the decoration. On either side of the windows just above the uppermost cornice, deep holes were cut into the walls (discovered during the 1980–89 restoration) to anchor short wooden brackets extending slightly beyond the cornice. A wooden beam was then laid horizontally across these two brackets to support a wooden truss or scaffold wider than the window. This truss arched across the space to the corresponding beam and brackets on the opposite wall. Much like the scaffold used in the recent restoration (fig. 8), it was probably stepped to conform to the

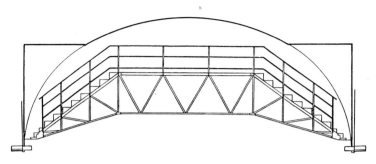

Fig. 8 - Cross-section diagram of the scaffold used in the 1980-89 restoration of the Sistine ceiling

curvature of the vault. This allowed Michelangelo to work on most sections of the ceiling in a standing position. These trusses were placed in six positions—one over each pair of opposing windows on the long walls—mirroring the paired ribs of the ceiling's painted architecture. They were probably connected to each other by means of movable planks. It is not known how many trusses were constructed at one time, perhaps three, perhaps all six. If all six trusses were installed at the beginning, the noisiest and dirtiest part of the project could have been concentrated into a single brief period. They would have allowed the previous decoration to be chiseled away at one time and the entire surface to be prepared with *arriccio,* a rough plaster layer of lime and *pozzolana* (powdered volcanic rock) designed to support the *intonaco,* a finer plaster layer of the same materials, which Michelangelo applied in small patches and painted while still wet. During the painting of the vault, however, probably only two or three of the trusses were inter-

connected by planks at any one time to allow as much light as possible to reach the ceiling. Michelangelo, in any case, painted from the entrance wall through the *Creation of Eve,* including the lunettes, in a first campaign from May 1508 to August 1510 and the remainder in a second from sometime in 1511 to 31 October 1512, when completion of the entire chapel was celebrated at vespers on the vigil of All Saints' Day.

This order of execution runs contrary to the narrative progression discussed later in this essay. Michelangelo perhaps intuited that his vision would grow in the course of painting the ceiling, so he saved the sublime acts of God's creation for last.

The recent restoration has provided an exact picture of Michelangelo's techniques. In spite of some initial difficulties with mold or salt efflorescence appearing on the *intonaco* reported by Vasari, and Michelangelo's own feelings of frustration, anxiety, discomfort, fatigue, and even incompetence reported in complaining letters to his father and in a burlesque sonnet to a friend, the visual evidence shows that Michelangelo, who learned traditional fresco techniques as an apprentice with Domenico Ghirlandaio in Florence, was a superb technician.

Michelangelo employed a total of thirteen *garzoni,* or assistants, eight continuously. They helped to prepare the scaffolding and the surface of the vault, transport supplies, mix plaster, grind pigments, lay out and transfer designs, and paint decorative details such as the architecture, swags, minor secondary figures, and lettering. But Michelangelo executed the bulk of the ceiling substantially alone, an unprecedented achievement considering that the design incorporates more than 380 figures on more than 12,916 square feet (1,200 square meters) of surface.

Michelangelo first made small compositional and figural studies in ink and chalk. These he elaborated into full-size drawings, called cartoons, which he used for many parts of the ceiling. After he had perforated the outlines of the figures with a spiked pounce wheel, he carefully placed the cartoons against the wet *intonaco* and lightly pounced the perforated lines with a cloth bag filled with powdered carbon, leaving a carbon dust deposit of fine dotted lines, often still visible today in the hardened *intonaco*. Where detail was less important, in the drapery, for example, Michelangelo also used a faster method of tracing over the cartoon with a metal stylus, leaving a still-visible incised line in the wet *intonaco* to guide his painting. Besides these two indirect methods of transfer, Michelangelo also incised the *intonaco* directly with a stylus using nails, string, ruler, square, and compass to lay out the painted architecture and the medallions. On occasion, he also sketched designs in sinopia directly on the *arriccio* to help delimit the size and shape of *intonaco* plastered on any given day. This area of *intonaco* is called a *giornata* (a day's work, although several *giornate* might be done on a single day), each of which is still visible today by the overlap formed between successive patches of plaster.

Once the *intonaco* was in place and the design transferred, Michelangelo sometimes further defined a contour with a black or brown line of pigment. He then brushed his colored pigments mixed with water onto the *intonaco* often "sculpting" foreground forms with a dense network of hatched, chisel-like brushstrokes. Background figures were usually more sketchily painted with broader, more liquid strokes. To compensate for the relatively dim natural light and the great height of the vault, Michelangelo used brilliant colors, sometimes boldly juxtaposed in startling contrasts, sometimes subtly superimposed like glazes to create transparencies, but always deployed to help define form three-dimensionally. All this required great skill and sureness of touch because not only did pigments look different wet than dry, but once the pigments soaked into the *intonaco*, no changes were possible owing to a process of chemical bonding with the plaster that transformed them into a durable calcium carbonate.

Up to this point the process was known as *buon fresco*, or true fresco. But Michelangelo occasionally went back later to make minor corrections on the hardened *intonaco*, using pigments mixed with a binding agent such as animal glue and oil. In the case of the medallions and a few other areas, he applied gold leaf with a resin-and-oil size. Since pigments in this so-called dry, or *a secco*, technique were not bonded with the wet *intonaco*, they could flake off, as has happened in places, especially on the medallions. But the great success of the recent cleaning is largely due to the fact that Michelangelo worked very little *a secco*.

As Michelangelo became more confident and sure, he became bolder. In the first campaign, he consistently used the pounce bag and only occasionally the stylus for the transfer of designs. In the second campaign, the situation was reversed with designs ever more summarily indicated. Similarly, in the early phases, the *giornate* were relatively small and numerous—for example, twenty-nine for the *Flood*, eleven for the *Drunkenness of Noah*. In the later phases the *giornate* grew increasingly larger and fewer—seven for the *Creation of Sun, Moon, and Plants* and one for the *Separation of Light and Dark*. From the beginning, however, Michelangelo executed all the lunettes, most of the fictive bronze nudes above the spandrels and pendentives, and a few other minor figures, using no cartoons at all, although he certainly had made small studies and probably sketched out these areas in sinopia on the *arriccio*.

STRUCTURE OF THE CEILING DECORATION[9]

If Pier Matteo d'Amelia's design accurately depicts the fifteenth-century state of the ceiling, Michelangelo cut away masonry in three areas: the acanthus capitals at the tops of the pilasters between the windows; the horizontal ribs above the coats of arms at either end; and the diagonal ribs separating the eight corner spandrels, which transformed them into four pendentives (compare fig. 5 and plate 1). These subtle but important changes provided greater unity by making the curved surface of the vault more taut and integrated and by making the transition between the walls and lunettes more flowing and continuous.

When Michelangelo began the Sistine Chapel project, the most popular designs for frescoed vaults in Rome were derived from ancient Roman painted and stuccoed vaults first discovered in the late 1480s. A drawing in Siena by Giuliano da Sangallo (c. 1445–1516), inscribed in Italian "the compartmentation of an ancient vault in Rome,"

gives an excellent impression of such layouts (fig. 9). It was adapted, for example, by Raphael for the vault of the Stanza della Segnatura in the Vatican, commissioned about 1508 by Julius II (fig. 10), and by Pinturicchio for the choir vault of Santa Maria del Popolo, at almost the same time in another Julian commission. These designs *all'antica* were characterized by complex geometrical patterns emphasizing the surface and enclosure of the vault, not its structure.

Michelangelo's first conception of the ceiling with compartments of circles, squares, and rectangles, recorded in a drawing in the British Museum, was inspired by such designs *all'antica* (figs. 11, 12). The commission, it will be recalled, initially called for the Twelve Apostles. Michelangelo thus envisioned twelve thrones in niches flanked by winged angels and volutes within the triangular spaces above the pilasters where the vault joined the walls—thrones that

Fig. 9 - Giuliano da Sangallo, *Ancient Roman Vault* (from Hadrian's Villa at Tivoli), drawing, Siena, Biblioteca Comunale

Fig. 10 - Raphael, vault, fresco, Vatican, Stanza della Segnatura, c. 1508

Fig. 11 - Michelangelo, *First Design for the Sistine Ceiling*, London, British Museum

Fig. 12 - Reconstruction of Michelangelo's first design for the Sistine ceiling

eventually evolved into seats for the prophets and sibyls in the final design. A cornice, broken by the thrones, ran along the tops of the lunettes and bounded the main longitudinal field. A square turned 45 degrees to form a diamond linked the two opposing thrones and mediated between transverse and longitudinal axes of the vault.

Thinking as a sculptor in terms of load and support, Michelangelo made this scheme more lucid and architectural in a second drawing now in Detroit (figs. 13, 14). He lowered the throne niches to avoid breaking the cornice and created a clearer tripartite scheme. The design thus more effectively related to the three horizontal bands dividing the walls below. He also made the transverse axes stronger and more structural by thickening the pilasters of the thrones to support the cornice and by adding paired ribs that spring from them. The cornice breaks out over the pilasters to form pseudocapitals that further emphasize the transverse axes without compromising the longitudinal one. Michelangelo simplified the central longitudinal area by replacing the diamonds with rectangles and the remaining geometrical fields with a large octagon. He was then only a few short steps away from the final design of alternating

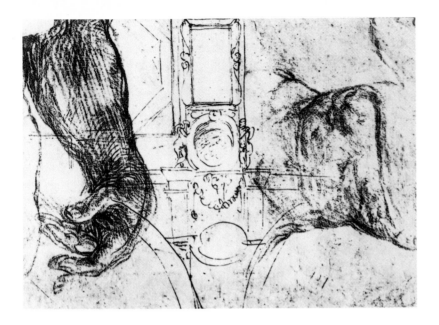

Fig. 13 - Michelangelo, *Second Design for the Sistine Ceiling,* Detroit Institute of Arts

Fig. 14 - Reconstruction of Michelangelo's second design for the Sistine ceiling

large and small rectangular fields (see Pl. 1). The standing winged angels in front of the paired ribs supporting medallions are also close to what became the seated nudes, or, as they are usually called in Italian, *ignudi*.

Michelangelo's final design is more directly related to the actual structure of a barrel vault (figs. 15, 16). As the degree of curvature in a barrel vault increases toward the walls, so too does the intensity of pressure pushing out against them. By a construction technique known as masonry loading, the walls are prevented from being pushed over by keeping the masonry relatively thin at the crown and making it increasingly thick toward the walls in order to convert by sheer dead weight outward thrust to downward pressure. The thrones of the prophets and sibyls—solid, massive, and rectilinear constructions replacing the earlier curved niches and seemingly excavated from the very thickness of the vault—respond to this area of greatest loading.

The transverse ribs springing from the pilasters of the thrones have become wider and thicker than those shown in the Detroit drawing, thereby creating stronger boundaries for the narratives and expressing more adequately the lateral forces of the barrel vault pushing

Fig. 15 - Michelangelo, Sistine ceiling, detail.

Fig. 16 - Diagram of Michelangelo's final design for the Sistine ceiling

26

Fig. 17 - Giotto, Scrovegni Chapel, fresco, Padua, c. 1305

A barrel vault encloses a longitudinal space that Michelangelo defined by the continuous cornice of his design. He gave this space a regular syncopated rhythm by the alternation of large and small narrative fields—a visual counterpart to the stately procession of the *capella papalis* into the *sancta sanctorum*. There is, however, a dramatic tension between the chronological arrangement of the frescoes from altar to entrance and the movement of the *capella papalis* down the processional axis from entrance to altar. Michelangelo intensified this tension by facilitating a reading of the vault in a single sweeping glance from altar to entrance when entering. The histories farthest away are easier to read with fewer, larger, more active figures. Similarly, the prophets and sibyls increase in size toward the altar—the Delphic Sibyl, for example, is approximately 12 feet 8 inches (3.86 meters) tall, the Cumæan 13 feet 11 inches (4.25 meters), and the Libyan 14 feet 11 inches (4.54 meters).

Ignudi seated on cubic blocks mediate the intersections between Michelangelo's transverse and longitudinal systems where the ribs and cornice meet. The sheer strength and vibrancy of the *ignudi* express anatomically the architectural work the ribs seem to perform shouldering the weight of the vault. They also help to define the longitudinal system's running cornice as they lean diagonally forward or back, pulling on ribbons attached to the medallions. Finally, in cooperation with the *cancellata*, the *ignudi* focus attention on the central bay with the *Creation of Eve* (fig. 18). Here, and only here, all four *ignudi* lean

out against the walls. The addition of pseudomarble infants carved from the piers of the thrones—derived from classical putti, but here most unusually paired males and females—gives the impression of their relating to these forces by actively carrying the cornice like caryatids. The pairs of ribs and pilasters suggest accurately that the lateral forces of the vault are not uniform along the walls but instead directed around the windows onto the piers by means of the spandrels, pendentives, and lunettes. Earlier vaults sometimes featured painted ribs expressing lateral forces—for example, Giotto's vault in the Scrovegni Chapel in Padua of c. 1305 (fig. 17)—but none was as logical, consistent, and structural as Michelangelo's design.

Fig. 18 - Michelangelo, *Creation of Eve* and surrounding *ignudi*, Sistine Chapel ceiling

Fig. 19 - Arch of Constantine, Rome, A.D. 312-315

inward in an X-shaped configuration reinforcing the crossed diagonals of the scene's composition. Michelangelo's layout appears solid and sculptural. However, it never seriously compromises the ceiling's quality of flat enclosure. The ribs are three layers thick, but the layers are defined by shadow without perspective and thus adhere to the surface. In the narrative fields, the figures are close to the surface and the spaces they occupy shallow, even when intended to suggest cosmic vastness. The cubes on which the *ignudi* sit are curiously planar, all lines of recession masked by legs or drapery. Short or obscured orthogonals even deprive the thrones of the prophets and sibyls of much perspective depth.

A closer look at the architectural logic of the design also raises questions. The paired ribs and pilasters of the thrones are not aligned with the single pilasters on the walls. The seers' footrests, which are the only elements of the design with relatively long lines of perspectival recession, seem to detach the thrones from the wall and project them into the space of the chapel. This effect is intensified by infants yoked to signboards who hang from, rather than support, the footrests (see page 39). The rams' skulls linking the spandrels and the cornice provide little structural support. And most important, at each end of the central section a thin strip of blue sky can be seen beyond the ribs (see Plate 1).

These patches of sky reveal that, just as in Pier Matteo d'Amelia's design, the whole is a hovering celestial vision.

Michelangelo, in short, has to an unprecedented degree developed and transcended the tradition of an architectonic vault design in response to the structure of the chapel. In a masterfully balanced synthesis, however, he has incorporated within his design the contradictory traditions of a nonstructural geometrically inscribed surface and an enclosureless heavenly apparition. Michelangelo also recalled and archaeologically updated the fifteenth-century triumphal-arch motifs formed by the windows flanked by painted niches with the popes, when he imaginatively recombined in his design the major elements of the Arch of Constantine (fig. 19). The victories on the arch's column plinths mirror Michelangelo's innocents on the seers' thrones; the paired columns, the paired ribs; and the river gods and victories above the arches, the bronze nudes above the spandrels and pendentives. The seasons represented below the central arch's winged victories correspond to Michelangelo's infants yoked to signboards; the round reliefs, to the medallions; and the narrow frieze below the round reliefs, to the fifteenth-century frescoes on the walls. The barbarian kings standing on cubic bases above the columns relate to the *ignudi*, and the large reliefs in the attic, to the central narratives. These references to the Arch of Constantine connote the triumph of an imperial church, a crucial aspect of the entire chapel's decoration. The strong accents of imperial purple, especially evident on the robes of God, a stand-in for Julius II, reinforce the sense of triumphalism.

STRUCTURE OF THE CENTRAL NARRATIVES

Nine central narratives from Genesis (Plate 1, fig. 1) represent the era *ante legem* (before the law of Moses). They thus properly precede the two cycles of fifteen-century frescoes on the walls from the eras *sub lege* (under the law of Moses) and *sub gratia* (under the grace of Christ). They are also arranged chronologically—with two transpositions explained in the commentary on the central narratives—from altar to entrance following the arrangement of the wall frescoes. Subdivided into three groups with three scenes each—stories of the Creation, Adam and Eve, and Noah—they alternate in a regular rhythm of small scene, large scene. This necessarily creates within the triads a syncopation that scans a-A-a, B-b-B, and c-C-c. This organization places particular emphasis on the central group with Adam and Eve, for it is the only triad with two large scenes.

The central scene of this middle triad, the *Creation of Eve* (fig. 18), was given particular prominence, as we saw in the previous section, by its X-shaped composition, by the inward-leaning, X-configured *ignudi* who surround it, and by its location over the *cancellata*. The *Creation of Eve* thus serves as a fulcrum dividing the narratives into two counterbalanced units. The first unit, appropriately over the *sancta sanctorum*, shows God in heaven creating the universe and the first human, still godlike before the Fall. The second, appropriately over the area outside the holy of holies, depicts sinful humankind on earth after the Fall in need of redemption by an incarnate savior.

Within this larger structure of diads—reflecting the two favorite themes of preachers of the *capella papalis,* the Creation and the Incarnation—three pairs of smaller diadic relationships exist. That is, each scene in one half of the vault relates responsively and contrapuntally in form and content to the corresponding scene in the other half—for example the *Drunkenness of Noah* at one end to the *Separation of Light and Dark* at the other (figs. 20, 21)—as is developed in more detail in the commentary on the central narratives (see page 60).

This narrative structure directly mirrors Renaissance perceptions of the shape of Christian history. The chronological arrangement connotes a belief in a linear and sequential unfolding of events according to divine plan that unifies all space and time until the end of time. The diads suggest an experience of history, fundamental to Christian theological thought, as a struggle between binary opposites such as spirit and matter, heaven and earth, good and evil, sin and salvation, sinner and saint, or death and life. The triads imply the traditional scheme that subdivided history into the three eras—*ante legem, sub lege,* and *sub gratia*—in which the first two prefigured the third. They also relate to a Trinitarian vision of the universe with a three-part divinity. The first part (the Father) exists eternally and spiritually outside of space and time; the second (the Son) manifests itself materially at a specific moment of space and time; and the third (the Holy Spirit) flows continuously through history uniting spirit and matter through all space and time. The complexity and flexibility of such thinking guarantees that there can never be single, final, or correct interpretation of any biblical episode, but rather multiple, interconnected, overlapping, even conflicting possibilities. Furthermore, signs are polysemous, with meanings shifting according to cultural circumstances and to the culture individual viewers bring to them.

The commentary on the color plates that follows is thus intended to be suggestive not definitive. I have tried, however, to select possibilities that can be supported by the visual evidence and by my understanding of the Julian Age.[10]

Fig. 20 - *Drunkenness of Noah*

Fig. 21 - *Separation of Light and Dark*

Fig. 22 - *Flood*

Fig. 23 - *Creation of the Sun, Moon, and Plants*

Fig. 24 - *Sacrifice of Noah*

Fig. 25 - *Separation of Water from Firmament and Water Brings Forth Life*

Fig. 26 - *Temptation and Expulsion*

Fig. 27 - *Creation of Adam*

Fig. 28 - *Diomedes and the Palladium,* cast from lost carved chalcedony gem

Fig. 30 - Apollonios, *Torso Belvedere (Hercules),* Vatican Museums, c. 150 B.C.

Fig. 29 - Hagesandros, Polydoros, and Athanodoros of Rhodes, *Laocoön,* Vatican Museums, c. 20 B.C.-A.D. 20

[1] For the construction and fifteenth-century decoration of the chapel, see Eugenio Battisti, "Il significato simbolico della Cappella Sistina," *Commentari* 8 (1957): 96–104; L.D. Ettlinger, *The Sistine Chapel before Michelangelo. Religious Imagery and Papal Primacy* (Oxford, 1965); Rona Goffen, "Friar Sixtus IV and the Sistine Chapel," *Renaissance Quarterly* 39 (1986): 218–62; Carol F. Lewine, *The Sistine Chapel Walls and the Roman Liturgy* (University Park and London, 1993); Deoclecio Redig de Campos, "I 'tituli' degli affreschi del quattrocento nella Cappella Sistina," *Rendiconti della Pontificia Accademia Romana di Archeologia,* ser. 3, 42 (1969–70): 299–314 [also in *Studi di Storia dell'Arte in onore di Valerio Mariani* (Naples, 1971), 113–21]; Roberto Salvini, "The Sistine Chapel: Ideology and Architecture," *Art History* 3 (1980): 144–57; John Shearman, "The Chapel of Sixtus IV," in *The Sistine Chapel. The Art, the History, and the Restoration* (New York, 1986), 22–87; and idem, "La Storia della Cappella Sistina," in *Michelangelo e la Sistina. La tecnica, il restauro, il mito* (Rome, 1990), 19–28.

For Sixtus IV, see Egmont Lee, *Sixtus IV and Men of Letters* (Rome, 1978), and for Pier Matteo d'Amelia, see Federico Zeri, "Pier Matteo d'Amelia e gli Umbri a Roma," in *Dall'Albornoz all'età dei Borgia. Questioni di cultura figurative nell'Umbria meridionale* (Todi, 1990), 17–40.

[2] Perugino's altarpiece, the opening scene from the life of Moses *(Finding of Moses)* and from the life of Christ *(Nativity)* that flanked the altarpiece, and the depiction of the first four popes were all destroyed when Michelangelo painted his *Last Judgment* between 1536 and 1541. The rest of the decoration remains *in situ.* However, the last scene from the life of Moses *(Fight for Moses' Body)* and from the life of Christ *(Resurrection)* were repainted in the first half of the 1570s by Matteo da Lecce (Matteo Pérez de Alesio, c. 1547–1607/16) and Arrigo Fiammingo (Hendrik van den Broeck, c. 1530–1592/1605), when part of the east wall of the chapel collapsed.

[3] For the function of Sistine Chapel, see John Shearman, *Raphael's Cartoons in the Collection of Her Majesty the Queen and the Tapestries for the Sistine Chapel* (London, 1972), esp. 21–30; idem, "The Chapel of Sixtus IV," *The Sistine Chapel. The Art, the History, and the Restoration* (New York, 1986), 22–37; idem, "La Storia della Cappella Sistina," *Michelangelo e la Sistina. La tecnica, il restauro, il mito,* (Rome, 1990), 19–28.

Officials of the *capella papalis* included the pope, cardinals, heads of monastic orders, patriarchs, visiting archbishops and bishops, visiting sovereigns, ambassadors, the Senator and Conservators of Rome, the Prefect of Rome, Roman nobles, the papal theologian, the Master of Ceremonies, the sacristan, the major-domo, chamberlains, secretaries, notaries, auditors, the captain of the Swiss guard, servants of the cardinals, the papal choir, the celebrant priest, deacons, acolytes, and assorted others.

[4] For Michelangelo's commission see Giorgio Vasari, *La Vita di Michelangelo nelle redazioni del 1550 e del 1568,* 5 vols., ed. Paola Barocchi (Milan and Naples, 1962); Ascanio Condivi, *The Life of Michelangelo,* trans. Alice Sedgwick Wohl, ed. Hellmut Wohl (Baton Rouge, 1976); *The Letters of Michelangelo,* ed. E.H. Ramsden, 2 vols. (Stanford, Calif., 1963), esp. 1: 45–77, 148–50, and 240–46; John Shearman, "The Chapel of Sixtus IV," *The Sistine Chapel. The Art, the History, and the Restoration,* (New York, 1986), 32–33; and idem, "La Storia della Cappella Sistina," *Michelangelo e la Sistina. La tecnica, il restauro, il mito* (Rome, 1990), pp. 25–27.

[5] For the sacred oratory of Sistine through Julian Rome, see John W. O'Malley, "Preaching for the Popes," in *The Pursuit of Holiness in Late Medieval and Renaissance Religion,* ed. Charles Trinkaus and Heiko Oberman (Leiden, 1974), 408–40; idem, *Praise and Blame in Renaissance Rome. Rhetoric, Doctrine, and Reform in the Sacred Orators of the Papal Court, c. 1450–1521,* Duke Monographs in Medieval and Renaissance Studies, vol. 5 (Durham, N.C., 1979); and idem, "The Theology Behind Michelangelo's Ceiling," *The Sistine Chapel. The Art, the History, and the Restoration* (New York, 1986), 92–148.

[6] For Pope Julius II and his times, see John O'Malley, *Giles of Viterbo on Church and Reform. A Study in Renaissance Thought* (Leiden, 1968); Loren Partridge and Randolph Starn, *A Renaissance Likeness. Art and Culture in Raphael's "Julius II"* (Berkeley and Los Angeles, 1980); Loren Partridge, *The Art of Renaissance Rome, 1400–1600* (New York and London, 1996); Charles L. Stinger, *The Renaissance in Rome* (Bloomington, Ind., 1985); Marjorie Reeves, ed., *Prophetic Rome in the High Renaissance Period* (Oxford, 1992); and the extensive bibliographies in all five books.

[7] For general studies on Michelangelo, see Paul Barolsky, *Michelangelo's Nose. A Myth and Its Maker* (University Park and London, 1990); Herbert von Einem, *Michelangelo,* trans. Ronald Taylor (London, 1959); and Howard Hibbard *Michelangelo* (New York, 1974).

For Michelangelo's poetry, see James M. Saslow, *The Poetry of Michelangelo* (New Haven and London, 1991), esp. 70–72 for the burlesque poem written c. 1509–10 about painting the Sistine Chapel ceiling, including an autograph sketch showing Michelangelo "standing and craning his neck upward while painting a cartoonlike figure on the ceiling."

For Michelangelo's impact on other artists, see Sydney J. Freedberg, *Painting of the High Renaissance in Rome and Florence*, 2 vols. (Cambridge, Mass., 1961); Alida Moltedo et al., *La Sistina Riprodotta. Gli affreschi di Michelangelo dalle stampe del Cinquecento alle campagne fotografiche Anderson* (Rome, 1991); and Giovanni Morello, "La Sistina tra copie e incisioni," in *Michelangelo e la Sistina. La tecnica, il restauro, il mito* (Rome, 1990), 135–227.

For the social status of artists, see Michael Baxandall, *Giotto and the Orators: Humanist Observers on Painting in Italy and the Discovery of Pictorial Composition, 1350–1450* (Oxford, 1971); idem, *Painting and Experience in Fifteenth Century Italy* (Oxford, 1972); Peter Burke, *Culture and Society in Renaissance Italy, 1420–1540* (New York, 1972); E.H. Gombrich, "The Renaissance Conception of Artistic Progress and Its Consequences," in *Norm and Form. Studies in the Art of the Renaissance* (London, 1966), 1–10; R.W. Lee, "*Ut pictura poesis:* The Humanistic Theory of Painting," *Art Bulletin* 22 (1940): 197–269; Martin Wackernagel, *The World of the Florentine Renaissance Artist. Projects and Patrons, Workshop and Art Market*, trans. Alison Luchs (Princeton, 1981); Martin Warnke, *Hofkünstler. Zur Vorgeschichte des modernen Künstlers* (Cologne, 1985); and Rudolph Wittkower and Margot Wittkower, *Born under Saturn. The Character and Conduct of Artists* (London, 1963).

[8] For the scaffolds, campaigns, and techniques, see Creighton E. Gilbert, "On the Absolute Dates of the Parts of the Sistine Ceiling," *Art History* 3 (1980): 158–81 [reprinted in *Michelangelo, On and Off the Sistine Ceiling, Selected Essays* (New York, 1994), 191–224]; Frederick Hartt, Gianluigi Colalucci, Fabrizio Mancinelli, and Takashi Okamura, *The Sistine Chapel*, 2 vols. (New York, 1991), esp. 354–360; Frederick Hartt, *The Drawings of Michelangelo* (London, 1971); idem, "The Evidence for the Scaffolding of the Sistine Ceiling," *Art History* 5 (1982): 273–86; Paul Joannides, "On the Chronology of the Sistine Chapel," *Art History* 5 (1982): 250–53; Michael Hirst, "Gli studi per la Sistina, volta," Fabrizio Mancinelli, "Tecnica di Michelangelo e organizzazione del lavoro, ponteggio," and Gianluigi Colalucci, "Esecuzione pittorica," in *Michelangelo e la Sistina. La tecnica, il restauro, il mito* (Rome, 1990), 41–46, 55–64, and 69–84, respectively; Michael Hirst, "'Il modo delle attitudini': Michelangelo's Oxford Sketchbook for the Ceiling," and Fabrizio Mancinelli, "Michelangelo at Work: The Painting of the Ceiling," in *The Sistine Chapel. The Art, the History, and the Restoration* (New York, 1986), 208–17 and 218–59; Fabrizio Mancinelli, "Il ponte di Michelangelo per la Cappella Sistina," *Rassegna dell'Accademia Nazionale di San Luca* 1–2 (1982): 2–7; idem, "The Technique of Michelangelo as a Painter: A Note on the Cleaning of the First Lunettes in the Sistine Chapel," *Apollo* 117 (1983): 362–67; Charles de Tolnay, *Corpus dei disegni di Michelangelo*, 4 vols. (Novara, 1971–80); and William E. Wallace, "Michelangelo's Assistants in the Sistine Chapel," *Gazette des Beaux-Arts*, ser. 6, vol. 110 (1987): 203–16.

For the Japanese involvement in the 1980–89 restoration, see Waldemar Januszczak, *Sayonara, Michelangelo. The Sistine Chapel Restored and Repackaged* (Reading, Mass., and Menlo Park, Calif., 1990).

[9] For the structure of the vault, see Edmund R. Leach, "Michelangelo's *Genesis.* Structuralist Comments on the Paintings on the Sistine Chapel Ceiling," *Times Literary Supplement,* March 18, 1977, 311–13; Charles Robertson, "Bramante, Michelangelo and the Sistine Ceiling," *Journal of the Warburg and Courtauld Institutes* 49 (1986): 91–105; Sven Sandström, "The Sistine Chapel Ceiling," in *Levels of Unreality. Studies in Structure and Construction in Italian Mural Painting During the Renaissance* (Uppsala, 1963), 173–191; and Juergen Schulz, "Pinturicchio and the Revival of Antiquity," *Journal of the Warburg and Courtauld Institutes* 25 (1962): 35–55.

For the importance of the entrance or threshold view of vault decoration, in this case domes, but still relevant for the Sistine ceiling, see John Shearman, *Only Connect.…Art and the Spectator in the Italian Renaissance* (Princeton, 1992), 149–91.

[10] For interpretations of the ceiling, see Paul Barolsky, "Metaphorical Meaning in the Sistine Ceiling," *Source* 9 (1990): 19–22; James Beck, "Michelangelo's *Sacrifice* on the Sistine Ceiling," *Renaissance Society and Culture,* ed. John Monfasani and Ronald G. Musto (New York, 1991), 9–22; Malcolm Bull, "The Iconography of the Sistine Chapel Ceiling," *Burlington Magazine* 130 (1988): 597–605 (abridged in *Prophetic Rome in the High Renaissance Period,* ed. Marjorie Reeves (Oxford, 1992), 307–19; Esther Gordon Dotson, "An Augustinian Interpretation of Michelangelo's Sistine Ceiling," *Art Bulletin* 61 (1979): 223–56, 405–29; Patricia Emison, "Michelangelo's Adam, Before and After Creation," *Gazette des Beaux-Arts* 112 (1988): 115–18; Creighton E. Gilbert, "The Proportion of Women" and "The Ancestors," in *Michelangelo, On and Off the Sistine Ceiling, Selected Essays* (New York, 1994), 58–112 and 115–49; Harry Gutman, "Nicholas of Lyra and Michelangelo's Ancestors of Christ," *Franciscan Studies,* n.s. 4 (1944): 223–28; idem, "Religiöser Symbolismus in Michelangelos Sintflut Fresco," *Zeitschrift für Kunstgeschichte* 18 (1955): 74–76; Rab Hatfield, "Trust in God: The Sources of Michelangelo's Frescoes on the Sistine Ceiling," *Occasional Papers Published by Syracuse University, Florence, Italy* 1 (1991), 23 pp.; Frederick Hartt, "'Lignum vitae in medio paradisi.' The Stanza d'Eliodoro and the Sistine Ceiling," *Art Bulletin* 32 (1950), 115–45, 181–218; idem, "Pagnini, Vigerio and the Sistine Ceiling: A Reply," *Art Bulletin* 33 (1951): 263–73; Charles Hope, "The Medallions on the Sistine Ceiling," *Journal of the Warburg and Courtauld Institutes* 50 (1987): 200–204; Rudolf Kuhn, *Michelangelo: Die Sixtinische Decke. Beiträge über ihre Quellen und zu ihrer Auslegugn* (Berlin, 1975); John O'Malley, "The Theology behind Michelangelo's Ceiling," *The Sistine Chapel. The Art, the History, and the Restoration* (New York, 1986), 92–148; Fabrizio Mancinelli and Anna Maria De Strobel, *Michelangelo. Le lunette e le vele della Cappella Sistina, Liber Generationis Jesu Christi* (Rome, 1992); Jane Schuyler, "The Cabalistic Doctrine of the Deity Reflected in Two Genesis Scenes of Michelangelo's Sistine Ceiling," *SECAC [Southeastern College Art Conference] Review* 10 (1985): 238–46; idem, "The Left Side of God: A Reflection of Cabala in Michelangelo's Genesis Scenes," *Source* 6 (1986): 12–19; idem, "The Female Holy Spirit (Shekhinah) in Michelangelo's *Creation of Adam,*" *Studies in Iconography* 2 (1987): 111–36; idem, "Michelangelo's Serpent with Two Tails," *Source* 9 (1990): 23–29; Charles Seymour, Jr., ed., *Michelangelo: The Sistine Chapel Ceiling* (New York, 1972); Staale Sinding-

Larsen, "A Re-Reading of the Sistine Ceiling," *Acta ad Archaeologiam et Artium Historiam Pertinentia* (Institutum Romanum Norvegiae) 4 (1969): 143–57; Leo Steinberg, "Eve's Idle Hand," *Art Journal* 35 (1975/76): 130–35; idem, "Who's Who in Michelangelo's *Creation of Adam:* A Chronology of the Picture's Reluctant Self-Revelation," *Art Bulletin* 74 (1992), 552–66; Ernst Steinmann, *Die Sixtinische Kapelle,* 3 vols. (Munich, 1901, 1905); Charles de Tolnay, *Michelangelo. The Sistine Ceiling,* vol. 2 (Princeton, 1947); Johannes Wilde, "The Sistine Ceiling," *Michelangelo: Six Lectures,* ed. John Shearman and Michael Hirst (Oxford, 1978): 48–84; Edgar Wind, "The Crucifixion of Haman," *Journal of the Warburg Institute* 1 (1938): 245–48; idem, "Sante Pagnini and Michelangelo: A Study of the Succession of Savonarola," *Gazette des Beaux-Arts,* 6th ser., 26 (1944): 211–46; idem, "The Ark of Noah: A Study in the Symbolism of Michelangelo," *Measure* 1 (1950): 411–21; idem, "Typology in the Sistine Ceiling: A Critical Statement," *Art Bulletin* 33 (1951): 41–47; idem, "Maccabean Histories in the Sistine Chapel: A Note on Michelangelo's Use of the Malermi Bible," in *Italian Renaissance Studies: A Tribute to the late Cecilia M. Ady,* ed. E. F. Jacob (London, 1960), 312–27; and idem, "Michelangelo's Prophets and Sibyls," *Proceedings of the British Academy* 51 (1965): 47–84.

PLATE 1

The Sistine Chapel ceiling

previous page: The *Delphic Sibyl,* with surrounding scenes

The Central Narratives

Plate 2

The Separation of Light and Dark

(Genesis 1:3–5)

The *Separation of Light and Dark* (Genesis 1:3–5) on the first day of Creation (Plate 2) is the first scene chronologically and the last in order of Michelangelo's execution. It was often interpreted in the Renaissance as the eternal conflict between good and evil, and the triumph of truth over falsehood. Saint Augustine of Hippo (354–430) conceived of it as a sign of the creation and division of the clean and unclean angels. It also prefigured Christ's earthly struggle with the dark forces of sin and his triumphal ascent into eternal light. The scene was thus appropriately placed over the presbytery with the triangular zone of light closest to the altar, where Christ's Sacrifice for the Redemption of humankind was regularly reenacted in the Mass.

At the height of his powers near the end of the fresco campaign, Michelangelo here represents God as having both the dynamism of youth and the wisdom of age. His God has masculine strength and, as signaled by the developed breasts, feminine fecundity. Omniscient and omnipotent, he contains complete within himself the principles of conception and creation. He is a titanic humanoid of far too unearthly anatomical power and grandeur to be containable within the cosmic field. He rotates through time along a diagonal axis in a double helix, like some huge galactic force in process of formation.

PLATE 3

THE CREATION OF SUN, MOON, AND PLANTS

(Genesis 1:11–19)

*T*he *Creation of Sun, Moon, and Plants* (Genesis 1:11–19), the first triad's largest scene (Plate 3), is out of chronological order with respect to the next scene. Within the scene itself, however, the normal reading order from left to right properly sequences the acts of the third and fourth days. But the fourth day's creation of the sun and moon is much more strongly emphasized than the third day's creation of plants. The vast sun near the center—its dazzling luminosity intensified by an angel shading his eyes—and God's massive figure on the right—enhanced by his accompanying angels, sweeping drapery, rocketlike trajectory, and magisterial double-armed creative gesture—visually overpower the smaller, solo figure of God on the left, who recedes and gestures with a single hand. The reason is clear. The sun was a common Renaissance symbol of the divine light of Christ, the *sol iustitiae,* or sun of justice. The moon, which reflects the radiance of the sun, was an emblem of the Virgin Mary, embodiment of the church. The scene thus prefigures Christ's Incarnation and the institution of the church. Like a theological diagram, the sun (the invisible church) takes priority over the moon (the visible church), and both outshine the plants (which suggest the church's spiritual fertility).

PLATE 4

THE SEPARATION OF WATER FROM FIRMAMENT
AND WATER BRINGS FORTH LIFE
(Genesis 1:6-8, 20-23)

The triad's final scene remains ambiguous (Plate 4). It could be a rare representation of God's spirit moving over the waters before the creation of days (Genesis 1:2). Given the chronological organization of all the narratives in the chapel, however, it more logically depicts the separation of water from firmament on the second day (Genesis 1:6–8). In his life of Michelangelo, Vasari called it the separation of land from water on the third day (Genesis 1:9–10), but he was probably wrong, because no land is depicted and a third-day event is shown in the preceding scene. Ascanio Condivi (1525–74), who is thought to have gotten his information directly from Michelangelo and to have written his life of Michelangelo to correct errors by Vasari, called it the creation of fish on the fifth day (Genesis 1:20–23). Even though no fish are shown, Condivi is surely partly right, since God's gesture implies "bringing forth" as much as "separating." Furthermore, an event from the fifth day would prepare for the next scene, the *Creation of Adam* on the sixth day. Thus the scene seems to combine two separate days of creation and is best titled the *Separation of Water from Firmament and Water Brings Forth Life*. Symbolically, fecund water suggested to Christian viewers the regenerative potential of baptism believed to cleanse the soul from the taint of original sin, just as God hovering over the water embodied the divine grace baptism was believed to channel to the faithful.

PLATE 5

THE CREATION OF ADAM

(Genesis 1:26–27; 2:7; 5:1–2)

The second triad's large opening scene, the *Creation of Adam* (Genesis 1:26–27; 2:7; 5:1–2), in fact, shows God channeling divine grace to the first human (Plate 5). By representing Adam's body as similar to God's in gesture, disposition, and might, Michelangelo shows Adam to be created in God's image and likeness. But Adam is also earth-bound and lethargic, essentially material. By contrast, God's spiritual essence is expressed by his billowing drapery against a backdrop of sky enfolding a multitude of angels and by his high-velocity, airborne movement toward Adam. God also has the mass, substance, and form of matter, just as Adam has the youth, beauty, and grace of spirit. More than simply the creation of Adam, then, Michelangelo has represented the moment when God by the touch of a finger will endow Adam with a soul, the moment when spirit and matter will conjoin. The fecundity of that junction is cued by the green color of the fluttering ribbon and the earth.

The scene also implies Christ's redemptive Incarnation, for Christ was commonly referred to as the second Adam (e.g., Romans 5:14; 1 Corinthians 15:22, 45–47). Thus, the woman under God's left arm, from whose loins the green drapery originates, was probably intended to be Eve, preordained from the beginning, and standard prefigura-tion of the Virgin, the vessel of Incarnation. If so, the robust child held by the two fingers of God's left hand—as a cel-ebrant priest would hold the Host—most probably prefigures the sacrificial Christ. Finally, Saint Augustine interpreted Adam's creation typologically as the Pentecost, the moment in which the church was sanctified by the Holy Spirit and given its mission to preach.

PLATE 6

THE CREATION OF EVE

(Genesis 2:20–25)

*T*he central triad's middle scene, the *Creation of Eve* (Genesis 2:20–25), is the fulcrum for the entire design, as we have seen (Plate 6). The scene's pivotal role was both deliberate and appropriate, for it was a common symbol of the founding of the church, embodied by the Virgin, the second Eve, just as the Virgin's Assumption, to which the chapel was dedicated, symbolized the church's triumph. Eve's importance is underlined by the mighty figure of God, cramped within the pictorial field, who appears for the first time standing on earth. Born from the side of Adam, Eve also alludes to the church's principal sacraments of baptism and the Eucharist, for both water and blood flowed from the side of Christ, the second Adam. And, indeed, Adam is intended to suggest the sacrificial Christ by his crumpled, sleeping figure leaning awkwardly against a dead, crosslike stump.

Plate 7

Temptation and Expulsion

(Genesis 3:1–24)

The central triad's last scene, the *Temptation and Expulsion* (Genesis 3:1–24), illustrates humankind's original sin and consequent Fall from grace, which necessitates Christ's Redemption (Plate 7). On the left a youthful Adam and Eve inhabit a green Garden of Eden. They exercise their free will, reaching toward the beautiful serpent-tailed female coiled around the tree of knowledge to accept the forbidden fruit. The fruit, however, is not shown. Their unified actions, expectant expressions, and young, powerful, interrelated bodies suggest a potentially fecund couple. Yet the absent fruit and the clawlike hands that seem to withhold or reject as much as to offer or accept hint at mental anxiety and conflict. The shadow on Adam's face, the barren rock, and the dead stump near Eve, echoing her fateful gesture, foretell imminent discord and death. Adam's eager reaching toward, and face-to-face confrontation with, the serpent, whom he resembles in features and hair color, show him to be as guilty as Eve. Eve, however, even more closely resembles the woman-serpent in face, body, and movement, as if she were the locus of evil. Further, her reclining posture as Adam lunges over her, her head at the level of his genitals, and the sexual connotations implicit in the configuration of her right hand all seem to suggest the widespread misogynist belief that female sexuality was the cause of the Fall.

The sexual anxieties of Michelangelo, perhaps a latent, if not an active, homosexual, might also be expressed here as well.

The sloping ground on the left draws the eye toward the right where the angel, in responsive counterpoint to the serpent, drives Adam and Eve from Paradise to the barren world beyond as they are linked lockstep in common guilt. The disharmony and death that their future now holds is signaled by bodies more aged and less graceful, bodies juxtaposed but disunited in physical and psychic response: Eve turns toward the angel but cowers in shadowed shame; Adam turns away from the angel's radiance but reaches out to ward off the sword. Yet the greening ground beneath their feet, the general cross-shaped composition, and the decisive grasp of a green limb by Adam, the Christ-type, foretell the coming Crucifixion and its promise of salvation. This reading gives point to a suggestion that the most unusual posture of Adam was based on a Greco-Roman relief of Hercules in the company of one of the Hesperides plucking an apple from their tree, known from a drawing by the artist and antiquarian Pirro Ligorio (c. 1500–83).[1] Hercules, a mortal who achieved immortality through his self-sacrificial labors, was commonly understood in the Renaissance as a type of Christ, and the garden of the Hesperides, a metaphor for Paradise.

PLATE 8

THE SACRIFICE OF NOAH

(Genesis 8:19–21; 9:1–19)

The *Sacrifice of Noah* (Genesis 8:19–21; 9:1–19) opens the third triad (Plate 8). It shows Noah in the central background, his wife to his left, and the Ark behind them, its door open. In front of the sacrificial altar are Noah's three sons. One to the left leads in a sacrificial ram; the next, on his hands and knees, tends the altar's fire; the third straddles a ram with its throat slit and twists around, handing to the wife of one of the sons the ram's blood-red entrails for sacrifice.[2] Another son's wife carries in a supply of wood, while the third, to Noah's right, dressed in green, places a sacrifice on the burning altar. This scene is out of chronological sequence with the next scene, the *Flood,* because here Noah and his family give thanks for the end of the flood. Here also God made his covenant, promising never again to destroy humankind by a flood and commanded Noah's sons and wives to increase and multiply to repopulate the earth.

Noah's Ark was a traditional medieval and Renaissance symbol of the church and its wood a sign of the Cross of the Crucifixion. The scene thus typologically prefigured the Mass, which reenacted the death of Christ and promised salvation. Christ, who was often called the Lamb, replaced the ram and henceforth made blood sacrifices such as Noah's unnecessary and unacceptable.

It is significant in this regard that both Condivi and Vasari insist that the scene represents the sacrifice of Cain and Abel. Although clearly incorrect, they are accurate in underlining the typological opposition between unacceptable and acceptable offerings. This opposition is here subtly enacted by the conflicting gestures of Noah, who points heavenward in anticipation of Christ's acceptable sacrifice, and the son's wife to his right, who recoils from what will become unacceptable.

The animals from the Ark may also be symbolic. The ox and ass, standard attributes of Christ's Nativity, signify the faithful Gentiles, who accepted Christ, in contrast to the Jews, who rejected him (Isaiah 1:3). The horse, for Giles of Viterbo, was an emblem of the church. The elephant was a classical sign of wisdom and, in the popular fourth- or fifth-century Latin translation of *Physiologus,* of Christ himself.

THE FLOOD

(Genesis 6, 7, and 8:1–14)

The triad's large middle scene, the *Flood* (Genesis 7:17–24; 8:6–8; more fully Genesis 6, 7, and 8:1–14), was the first to be executed (Plate 9). Michelangelo must almost immediately have recognized that it was too overloaded with figures to be easily read from the floor far below, because none of the subsequent narratives is so complex in structure or dense in meaning.

The composition is based on a series of contrasts that serve as a structural grid for the narrative's paradoxes of typological significance. An unstable tublike boat drifts in rough water in the center. Inside the flimsy vessel, six desperate windblown passengers try to make their escape. Two of the lost souls demonstrate the kind of inhumanity and cruelty that brought on the Flood in the first place. They violently drive out with fist and club a person trying to climb aboard and threaten to swamp the boat in the process. Ironically, the taint of original sin they enact will ultimately be cleansed by the sacrament of baptism, commonly symbolized by the flood waters.

In contrast to the tub, the solid Ark floats stably on calm water as ten windswept individuals either help each other climb onto its outer rim or attempt to enter by using a ladder and an ax. Although, according to the biblical story, these persons will drown, their charity toward their companions in distress suggests symbolically what was necessary to gain access to the church and its promise of regeneration.

And the Ark is one of the oldest symbols of the church, here under-lined by the symbolic dove of the Holy Spirit on top. On the Ark's right side, Noah marks the storm's end by welcoming not the usual dove but a cloud-covered sun. By this substitution, Michelangelo surely intended a reference to Ecclesiasticus (Sirach) 24:6–7, where Wisdom, the cloud covering the sun, was understood as an image of the Virgin, the vessel of the Incarnation.

Within the group on the right, a younger moribund man is carried by an older one, who appears to be his father (Plate 11). More to the right, a youthful man, supported by a companion dressed in green, seems to be dying. Both recall images of the dead Christ. Death and infertility are also expressed by the barren outcropping of rock with its flimsy tentlike shelter attached to a dead stump and by the helpless gestures, ineffectual actions, and despairing expressions of the figures within the tent. In addition, there are no unambiguous male/female couples within this group. Yet the wine keg in the center flanked by the two Christlike figures symbolizes the Eucharist, and the green draperies and green tree to the left, the rejuvenation it promises. (The green tree, and the *ignudo* just above, were mostly destroyed when a powder magazine exploded in the Castel Sant'Angelo in 1797, causing a large triangular patch of fresco to fall.)

The eye is led from the lower right toward the upper left by the composition's diagonal structure in both two and three dimensions. In the process, the activity of the left-hand group unfolds in strong contrast to the passivity of the right-hand group. These figures vigorously try to save themselves by climbing a green hill. As if preparing for the renewal of family life, a woman and two male companions carry an upturned stool, kitchen utensils, and two large bundles of personal effects. At the top of the hill, a nude women with blue-green drapery blowing around her in graceful curves holds one child while another grasps her thigh (Plate 10). She personifies charity or love of humankind, following a well-known visual prototype. This reading is supported by the tender ac-tions of the figures who flank her—a man carrying his spouse to the right and a couple embracing to the left. At the lower left, by contrast, an older nude women, who reclines on the ground, her breasts sagging and her leg draped over a severed tree stump, appears unable or unwill-ing to give nurture or comfort to the crying child behind her. This figure—a kind of inversion of the classical image of the fecund river god—is a stark reminder that all these energetic, caring people are doomed to die. The potential for salvation, however, is cued by four signs: the wood of the Ark, a usual symbol of Christ's Cross; the image of a youth with wind-filled drapery clinging to a dead tree with a sev-ered branch, which recalls the scene of the Crucifixion; the group of the ass, woman, child, and old bearded man to the extreme left, which refers to images of the Holy Family's flight into Egypt, always understood as a prefiguration of Christ's Sacrifice; and the bread on the upturned stool, which evokes the Eucharist, especially in view of its vertical alignment with the cloud-covered sun, sign of the Incarnation.

PLATE 10 - *The Flood,* detail

PLATE 11 - *The Flood,* detail

PLATE 12

THE DRUNKENNESS OF NOAH

(Genesis 9:20–27)

*T*he *Drunkenness of Noah* (Genesis 9:20–27), the third triad's last scene, shows the sleeping Noah on a gold-green cloth within a roofed shed shamefully drunk after testing the new vintage (Plate 12). His son Ham mocks him with a pointing gesture, while Shem and Japheth, both dressed in green drapery, avert their gazes. One of them piously covers Noah's nudity with a blue cloth.

Noah's fall was often understood as a second Fall of humankind, his sleep an allegory of death, and his mocking a prefiguration of Christ's mocking. Similarly, Noah's planting of the vine in the background suggests Christ's Incarnation; the wine vat, Christ's sacrifice; the pitcher and drinking cup, the Eucharist's vessels.

Michelangelo, as mentioned in the section discussing the structure of the central narratives, seems to have designed each scene in one half of the vault to respond to, as well as to contrast with, the corresponding scene in the other half, although this is somewhat obscured by his enormous stylistic development from the first narrative to the

last. The *Drunkenness of Noah* and the *Separation of Light and Dark* (figs. 20, 21, page 31) both feature powerful older men close to the picture surface composed on diagonals with areas of light and dark. These compositional similarities are appropriate, because both scenes allude to the promise of salvation through Christ's Incarnation, Sacrifice, and Resurrection. But the two scenes are also visually contrasted. Noah is unconscious and impotent, his sons' gestures reveal or cover sin within a dark and shallow interior space. God, by contrast, is supremely creative and potent as he pushes back the dark to reveal the light within the infinite cosmos. These formal dissimilarities are also apt because of differences in primary content. The *Drunkenness of Noah* emphasizes the Fall of humankind into sin, the *Separation of Light and Dark*, the triumph of good over evil.

The figures in the *Flood* and the *Creation of Sun, Moon, and Plants* (figs. 22, 23, page 31) are both composed along two parallel but opposed diagonals. The right-hand diagonal in the *Flood* (comprising the figure groups with the wine cask, tub, and Ark) runs from

foreground to background; the corresponding diagonal in the *Creation of Sun, Moon, and Plants* (formed by God and the sun and moon in the process of being created by him), from background to foreground. For the left-hand diagonals, the directions are reversed in each scene. Both scenes also feature the sun in the upper center of the composition. In the *Flood,* however, it is weakly shining through clouds in the background; in the *Creation of the Sun, Moon, and Plants,* it is brilliantly radiant in the foreground. In the *Flood,* the elements are out of control, provoking universal destruction. In the *Creation of the Sun, Moon, and Plants* the universe is being ordered by the regular cycle of night and day and the seasons. Again these formal responses and contrasts provide the structural scaffold for paradoxical symbolic meanings. One scene narrates the destruction of unenlightened humankind; the other, divine illumination. Both symbolize the foundation of the church, yet the *Flood* stresses the visible church—Christ's Passion and the sacraments of baptism and the Eucharist; in contrast, the *Creation of the Sun, Moon, and Plants,* highlights the invisible church—its eternal light and spiritual truth.

The *Sacrifice of Noah* and the *Separation of Water and Firmament* (figs. 24, 25, page 32) are both compact centralized compositions, but in the *Sacrifice of Noah,* the solid earthbound figures define a circular space as they move centrifugally around the cubic altar while attending to a rite of questionable acceptability. In the *Separation of Water and Firmament,* the airborne God and his two angelic companions hover in a dense ovoid mass expanding centripetally outward in an eternally valid act of fructifying the water. Symbolically the *Sacrifice of Noah* alludes to the Eucharist and, by the scurry of human devotional activity, the necessary act of cooperative free will. The *Separation of Water and Firmament* prefigures baptism and, by God's explosive creative power, his gift of grace independent of human will.

The Eucharist and baptism were the sacraments by which the church was believed to be built and salvation achieved. These scenes, thus, appropriately bracket the central triad with the Creation and Fall of humankind. This accounts for their chronological transpositions.

The *Temptation and Expulsion* and the *Creation of Adam* (figs. 26, 27, page 32) have similar triangular wedges of earth to the left and broad expanses of sky with a flying figure to the right. In the *Temptation and Expulsion,* the drama moves from left to right and the two groups of figures are sundered apart. In the *Creation of Adam,* the drama moves from right to left as the two groups conjoin. In the *Temptation and Expulsion,* Adam actively exercises his will (and lack of judgment), which results in his fall and death as God's grace is denied. In the *Creation of Adam,* Adam passively receives God's grace and the potential to act to merit it. Symbolically, the *Creation of Adam* alludes to Christ's Incarnation and promise of salvation—suggested by the stunning beauty and grace of his body. The *Temptation and Expulsion* prefigures Christ's Sacrifice—depicted by Adam's eager grasp of the tree and the cruciform composition.

THE PENDENTIVES

PLATE 13
DAVID AND GOLIATH

(1 Samuel 17:1–58)

PLATE 14
JUDITH AND HOLOFERNES

(Judith 13)

The two pendentives above the chapel's entrance wall (Plates 13, 14) represent *David and Goliath* (1 Samuel 17:1–58) and *Judith and Holofernes* (Judith 13). Here the Israelites are saved when hostile leaders are killed by individual acts of courage, typological allusions to Christ's Sacrifice and to the triumph of virtue over sin. The similarity in symbolic content is underlined by Michelangelo's compositions, which both counter the pendentive's curve forward at the sides and its retreat inward at the center. In *David and Goliath*, the eye is drawn back into space at the sides by Goliath's glance, his body's position, the sweep of the tent, and the placement of soldiers in the background. In *Judith and Holofernes*, this is achieved by Judith's glance and movement, the position of Holofernes's body, and the diagonal placement of the outside wall of Holofernes's bedroom. At the center of each scene, by contrast, the protagonists are projected forward against the inward-curving pendentive by the tent and the bedroom.

The narrative moment in each scene, however, is very different. In *David and Goliath*, David has dropped his slingshot in the foreground, straddled the felled giant, and twisted around like a coiled spring with one arm drawn back, the other steadying the Philistine's head. In just an instant the dramatic climax of the beheading will occur at the center of the composition. In *Judith and Holofernes*, the beheading has already occurred at the right, and Judith prepares to flee toward the left. Not surprisingly, greater visual prominence and drama are given to the typologically more important figure of David, the Christ-type par excellence. But Judith does act, if quietly. She covers the Assyrian general's head with a greenish cloth rather than placing it in a sack as the Bible recounts. This may be intended to prefigure the salvific Sacrifice of the Mass, in which the celebrant handles the Eucharist with veiled hands, a reading supported by a tradition that makes Judith a prototype for the Virgin. The depiction of Holofernes's chamber as solid architecture, in contrast to the Bible's location of the story in a tent, as if prefiguring the church, also favors such an interpretation.

PLATE 13 - *David and Goliath*

PLATE 14 - *Judith and Holofernes*

PLATE 15

THE BRAZEN SERPENT

(Numbers 21:4–9)

PLATE 16

THE DEATH OF HAMAN

(Esther 2, 3, 5, 7)

*I*n the opposite pendentives, the *Brazen Serpent* (Numbers 21:4–9) and the *Death of Haman* also illustrate deliverance of the Jewish people and symbolize salvation through Christ's Sacrifice (Plates 15, 16). When the Israelites rebelled against the hard desert life, God sent a plague of poisonous snakes to destroy them. When they repented, he instructed Moses to set up a serpent of brass on a pole and offered to cure the afflicted who looked upon it. Already in the gospel of John (3:14-15), this episode was understood as a prefiguration of the Crucifixion and its promise of salvation: "And just as Moses lifted up the serpent in the desert, so must the Son of Man be lifted up, so that everyone who believes in him may have eternal life." The event was also interpreted as a second Fall of humankind and often paired with a scene of the original sin. Michelangelo has, in fact, emphasized rebellion and sin. Fully two-thirds of the composition represents a dense mass of humanity in terror,

anguish, and pain as powerful bodies twist, writhe, and strain like vipers in a nest. The saved on the left include a woman, significantly recalling Eve of the *Temptation,* who lifts her left arm as she looks at the bronze serpent. Her snake-bitten right arm is raised by her crouching male companion, who, with strong overtones of sexuality, supports her between his legs and cups her breast from behind. Behind them stands a figure supporting a baby on his shoulder who reaches toward the bronze serpent. The couple and the baby express human sexual potency as a physical metaphor for the spiritual regeneration that the serpent/cross symbolizes. The remarkable absence of Moses—an antetype for the pope—would seem to connote the total dependence of the faithful on God's grace independent of the church's hierarchy. This extreme position remained possible for reformers in Julian Rome before lines hardened shortly thereafter when Protestants claimed the doctrine as theirs.

PLATE 15 - *Brazen Serpent*

The *Death of Haman* is a more complex narrative. Within the gate toward the right stands Mordecai, a Jew who served in the chancellery of King Ahasuerus of Persia. With him sits Esther, his cousin whom he had raised as an adopted daughter and who was now Ahasuerus's queen. Mordecai tells Esther that he had discovered a plot to kill the king and that she should warn the king, to whom he points. Although not shown, she does warn the king, whereupon the two conspirators are found out and hanged. The episode is later recorded in the chronicles of the king (Esther 2:19–23). Next—not represented but understood—the king names Haman his chief minister and bids all to kneel and bow down to him. Only Mordecai refuses to bow down (Esther 3:1–2). In revenge, Haman plans to kill all the Jews in the Persian Empire (Esther 3:3–15). Mordecai warns Esther of the plot and asks her to intercede with the king in order to save herself and the Jewish people (Esther 4). Then, as shown at the right of scene, Esther approaches the king, risking her life for appearing unbidden. She is well received and offered anything she desires by the king. She does not say what she desires at this time, but invites the king to a banquet she has prepared that day to entertain him and Haman (Esther 5:1–4).

The king and Haman attend the banquet, and Esther invites them to a second banquet for the next day where, she informs the king, she will reveal to him her wish (Esther 5:4–8). In the meantime, Haman—puffed up with more pride than ever because of the favor shown to him by the king and queen—prepares a gallows from which to hang Mordecai (Esther 5:9–14). Michelangelo has represented the gallows toward the center of the composition as a dead tree.

That very night the chronicles are read to Ahasuerus in his bedroom, and the king is reminded both of the treason that Mordecai had once discovered and his indebtedness to him (Esther 5:1–3). This may be the episode represented on the right in which the king is depicted stretched out on his bed with a servant reading a book rather than Esther's earlier visit (which in any case, according to the text, took place in the king's throne room, not bedroom). Or rather both events are probably intended to be recalled. Similarly, the king's commanding gesture may anticipate his order to punish Haman.

At the second banquet, shown to the left, Esther (seated to the left, crowned) reveals for the first time to the king (seated in the center) that she is Jewish. She concludes by reporting Haman's plot to massacre her people, and asks for deliverance. At this request Haman (seated to the right) recoils in fear of the king's anger (Esther 7:1–6).

After a short interval in which the king discovers Haman trying to rape Esther in revenge (adding an element of sexual assault as in the story of Judith), Haman is ordered hanged on the gallows that Haman himself had prepared for Mordecai (Esther 7:7–10). This crucifixion recalls Christ's Sacrifice in parallel with the brazen serpent opposite. Although Haman is guilty and Christ innocent, both sacrifices save an entire people.

Esther acts entirely within architectural space, and her actions

PLATE 16 - *Death of Haman*

in the narrative are primarily concerned with the ritual of the table. Consequently, she, like Judith diagonally across the ceiling, is a sign of the visible church and its rites at the altar table.

The *Death of Haman* depicts on the right loyal service and courage, on the left the revelation of betrayal and pride, and in the center just punishment. In responsive contrast, the *Brazen Serpent* shows punishment for disobedience and rebellion to the right, repentance and obedience to the left, and salvation in the center. The compositions serve as scaffolds that structure these similarities and differences in content. At the sides of the *Brazen Serpent,* which curve outward toward the viewer, are contrasted two outdoor episodes—violent implosive action to the right with a somewhat more subdued expansive movement outward to the left. As the pendentive recedes in the center, so the bronze serpent appears in the distance. At the sides of the *Death of Haman,* by contrast, indoor activities have been placed in the background in opposition to the forward curve of the field. At the right, the story expands slowly through time from foreground to background by a sequence of interrelated gestures, some seeming to perform double narrative duty. At the left, a decisive call for action is followed by an immediate reaction. In the center, Haman—with head and torso sharply turned in opposite directions, arms outstretched forward and back along a strong diagonal, his left leg drawn back and his right extended as if running—seems to explode into the pendentive's central void even though nailed to a tree. Common to both pendentives is the visual emphasis on sin and its punishment rather than virtue and its reward. This content and the violence with which Michelangelo has represented it may relate to the temper of the times, the years 1511–12 being the darkest moment in Julius II's reign.

THE PROPHETS AND SIBYLS

The Old Testament prophets and the ancient sibyls, it was believed, prepared the Jews and Gentiles for Christ's coming.[3] The Christian apologist Lactantius had collected the sibylline oracles in his *Divinae institutiones* of A.D. 304–11, and during the late Middle Ages and early Renaissance, sibyls had been frequently represented in art, especially in connection with the cult of Mary, since they were also virgins. But it was only in the fourth quarter of the fifteenth century with renewed interest in classical and early Christian writers that sibyls gained sufficient esteem to be represented on a monumental scale in chapel vaults traditionally reserved for patriarchs, evangelists, church fathers, and prophets. This development was spurred by the 1465 publication of the *Divinae institutiones* in Subiaco—the second book to be printed in Italy—and by a treatise on *I vaticini delle Sibille* published by the Dominican Filippo Barbieri as part of his larger

Opuscula in 1481 with several later editions. But it was first in the Sistine Chapel within the Vatican—thought to derive from the word *vaticini* (oracles)—that sibyls and prophets were represented on a vault together, as if, in the spirit of Lactantius, they held equivalent prophetic authority.

The prophecies of the Sistine seers treat, at length or fragmentarily, abundant and varied subjects that are often sufficiently obscure to offer nearly unlimited possibilities of interpretation. Those of *Zechariah* (Plate 17), who sits in profile leafing through a book above the entrance at one end of the chapel's longitudinal axis, prefigure almost the entire scheme of Christian Redemption including the Fall, the coming of a savior, his Passion, the triumph over evil, and salvation. Although flipping pages might suggest Zechariah's vast range of prophecies, here at the beginning of the decorative campaign nothing

PLATE 17 -*Zechariach*

PLATE 18 -*Jonah*

much beyond generic foreknowledge has been expressed. From here forward, however, Michelangelo's seers became increasingly explicit and forceful in significance.

Take *Jonah* (Plate 18), for example, with his strongly foreshortened whale at the opposite end of the vault over the altar. Jonah symbolized Christ's Entombment and Resurrection according to Matthew (12:40): "Just as Jonah was in the belly of the whale three days and three nights, so will the Son of Man be in the heart of the earth three days and three nights." As recounted in the Book of Jonah, however, the prophet here plays the role of sinner not savior. He disobeyed God's command to preach at Nineveh and tried to escape God's wrath by fleeing on a boat leaving from Joppa for Tarshish. This provoked both God's angry storm and the fear of the crew who threw him overboard. In his mercy, God rescued Jonah in a great fish. When Jonah repented his disobedience in the belly of the fish, God caused the fish to vomit him upon dry land (Jonah 1 and 2).

The green vine behind Jonah also refers to the prophet's rebellious spirit. When Jonah finally obeyed God and went to Nineveh, he prophesied that as a consequence of the inhabitants' wickedness the city would be destroyed. The people of Nineveh repented, however, and God saved the city. Resentful of appearing to be a false prophet, Jonah grew angry with God. This again incited God to demonstrate his power over the complaining prophet. One day he caused a gourd vine to grow for Jonah's shade and comfort and on the next caused it to wither so that the prophet became faint from the heat of the sun (Jonah 4:6–11).

Having just been regurgitated by the whale and seated in the soothing shade of the vine, Michelangelo's Jonah is both repentant sinner and recipient of God's grace. Thus, he appropriately links earth and heaven by gesturing downward toward the altar and looking upward to God in the *Separation of Light and Dark*. As a Jew who prophesied to the infidel Ninevites, Jonah's mediating gestures might also have been intended to suggest Christ's promise to reconcile all people. The need for reconciliation was implicit in the *Drunkenness of Noah* at the opposite end of the vault, for it was believed that Ham, cursed for mocking Noah, founded Nineveh, while Shem and Japheth, blessed for averting their gazes, founded, respectively, the Jewish and the Gentile peoples.

A valid alternative reading of *Jonah* interprets the whale as preparing to swallow the prophet and the vine about to wither. Michelangelo, in fact, has portrayed Jonah as more rebellious and apprehensive than repentant and blessed; this is shown by his shadowed face, anxious expression, ambiguous gestures, and precariously positioned body, which twists backward unstably along a diagonal, right foot suspended in the midair, left foot barely touching the throne by the tips of the toes. Without a book or scroll, Jonah is also defined more as actor than prophet, and the characters of the genii—one pensive, the other troubled—underline Jonah's conflicted sinner/savior role. This, in turn, relates to the dramatic struggle between sin and salvation played out in the flanking pendentives of the *Brazen Serpent* and the *Death of Haman.*

The remaining ten prophets and sibyls are arranged in cross-vault pairs similar to the fifteenth-century popes between the windows. *Jeremiah* (Plate 19) sits above the south wall to the left of the altar. He and his standing genii turn away from the altar toward a scroll to his right inscribed ALEF, the first letter of the Hebrew alphabet. This refers to Lamentations, whose five chapters are composed in acrostic form, each verse beginning with a different letter in alphabetical order. The Book of Lamentations mourns the sins of the Jews, the captivity of Palestine, and the destruction of Jerusalem. The laments were traditionally believed to foretell Christ's passion and were thus used in the Offices for Passiontide. Jeremiah is therefore appropriately near the *Death of Haman* and the dark side of the *Separation of Light and Dark.*

The enormous depths of his inner brooding and apocalyptic despair are communicated by the grief of his genii and by the closed silhouette of his massive, aged body, which seems almost to implode—ankles crossed and drawn back, head and shoulders hunched forward, left hand dangling limp in his lap, the right supporting his head and sealing the mouth of his shadowed face.

By contrast, the *Libyan Sibyl* (Plate 20) opposite is a figure of explosive vitality, her genii of inspiration engaged in animated conversation. The Libyan Sibyl (Libyca) sits facing the altar, her torso taut as a spring, with head, shoulders, and legs flat with respect to the back of the throne, as if about to spin around to slam shut her massive book of prophecy. Her twisted neck, extended muscular arms, sharply bent leg, arched feet, and flexed toes express great anatomical torsion and energy. Optical brilliance and rhythmic grace are conveyed by the sweeping drapery, vivid colors, and lively silhouette. This radiant and lithe figure closest to the light in the *Separation of Light and Dark* is the very embodiment her of prophecy of the coming illumination recorded in Barbieri's treatise of 1481: "Behold the day shall come, and the Lord shall lighten the thick darkness,…and they shall see the king of the living."

Both seers of the next pair, the *Persian Sibyl* (Plate 21) and *Daniel* (Plate 22), foretold the beasts of the Apocalypse heralding the Last Judgment. In addition, Daniel prophesied the Last Days, the four world empires, the Antichrist, and the triumph of a universal kingdom. For having survived the lion's den, he was also a symbol of Resurrection. From these rich possibilities, Michelangelo chose to limit his characterization of Daniel to the embodiment of renewed life in sharp contrast to the Persian Sibyl (Persica), the prophetess of dark destiny at the end of time.

She is old, seated in profile, back to the altar, face in shadow. He is young, seated frontally, leaning toward the altar, face illuminated. She myopically reads a small book, her genii passive. He actively

PLATE 19 - *Jeremiah*

PLATE 20 - *Libyan Sibyl*

PLATE 21 - *Persian Sibyl*

PLATE 22 - *Daniel*

writes, assisted by his genii, who watch over his shoulder and act as lectern for the large open book on his lap. Her form is closed, relatively small, and contained within the throne; her raised arms and bent legs animate her body, but her feet are lightly planted and her torso is relaxed. His form is huge and open, expanding beyond the confines of the throne; his feet are counterpoised, one forward and one drawn back; his upper torso turns and leans toward the left, alive with muscular tension. These connotations of life and regeneration opposing those of death and destruction are highly appropriate for the location of Daniel and Persica flanking the *Separation of Water from Firmament,* symbolic of baptism and God's grace.

The next pair, *Ezekiel* (Plate 23) and the *Cumæan Sibyl* (Plate 24), emphasize by their strong visual impact the principal transverse axis dividing the vault into halves. Ezekiel has just spun around from one genius—his scarf and scroll still rippling from the sudden movement—to carry on an intense polemic with the other angelically beautiful genius who points heavenward with both hands while Ezekiel's open-palm gesture equivocates between accepting and questioning. His extraordinary physical and rhetorical energy, second only to Jonah's, is heightened by the parallel diagonals of bull neck, thick torso, titanic limbs, and broad lavender drapery falling across his orange tunic and between his splayed knees.

The Cumæan Sibyl (Cumæa) has also twisted around on a diagonal to her right, but in contrast to Ezekiel's open form, hers is closed. Her feet and knees are pressed together, her eyes (and those of her genii) are focused on an elephant folio, which she supports with both hands, and her legs, torso, shoulders and right arm are knit together in a sweeping arabesque by the bright yellow drapery. By contrast to Ezekiel's oratorical force, she is an image of enormous inner concentration—and her massive bulk, Herculean arms, huge breasts, and luminous drapery imply a fertile intellect of exceptional brilliance and authority.

Most elite viewers within the Julian court would have understood immediately why these two seers, the only two with both feet firmly planted on their footrests, were singled out for particular emphasis and why they flanked the *Creation of Eve,* the crucially important symbol of the church's foundation. Ezekiel prophesied almost every concept important to Christianity: original sin and death (18:4), Virgin Birth (44:2), the Good Shepherd (34:23–24), redemptive baptism (36:25–26), Resurrection (37:1–14), and—especially important for Julius II as builder of New St. Peter's and renewer of the church—reconstruction and purification of the destroyed Temple of Jerusalem (40–48).

The Cumæan Sibyl (Cumæa) was the prophetess of the sun-god Apollo, and in Renaissance papal circles the home of the new Apollo, Christ, was the Vatican.[4] In Virgil's *Fourth Eclogue,* Cumæa foretold the virgin birth of a son who would bring a golden age, always understood by Christians as Christ's Incarnation and promise

PLATE 23 - *Ezekiel*

of salvation. Cumæa was often confused with the nymph Amalthea of classical mythology, who nursed the infant Jupiter, and thus could signify the Virgin who nurtured Christ. In Virgil's *Aeneid*, it was the Cumæan Sibyl who prophesied to Aeneas that, after a time of troubles, Emperor Augustus would bring triumph to his Julian clan and establish the *pax augusta*, the universal peace that Christians perceived as divine preparation for the *pax christi* founded at the moment of Christ's birth into Augustus's reign. And one of the major themes of propaganda in the court of Julius II was that of the pope as a new Augustus of the Julian line bringing to Italy, after an era of trials, a new millennial golden age. The imperial claims such propaganda promoted may account for the fact that Michelangelo has Cumæa, prophetess to the Gentiles, look West, and Ezekiel, prophet to the Jews, look East. In any case, the sibyls, in general, would seem to represent the church's universalism: Libyca personified Africa; Persica, the Holy Land; Cumæa, Italy; Erythræa, Asia; and Delphica, Greece.

The *Erythræan Sibyl* (Plate 25) and *Isaiah* (Plate 26) achieved fame because they prophesied so many events crucial to Christianity. The Erythræan Sibyl (Erithræa) foretold the presentation of Christ in the Temple, the calling of the apostles, the Apocalypse, and the Last Judgment; Isaiah foretold the Virgin Birth, Christ as the church's cornerstone, the church's foundation, and the church's mission to preach. Both were also understood to have foretold Christ's Incarnation, Passion, and Resurrection, and probably for this reason, they flank the

Sacrifice of Noah, which alludes to all three. According to tradition, Erythræa was even said to be Noah's daughter-in-law. She may be the woman in green in the *Sacrifice of Noah*, who, with a foreknowledge of the New Dispensation, recoils from the sacrifice of the Old.

Michelangelo treats the two seers almost as actors in a two-act play. *Act One*: Erythræa sits quietly in profile, right arm hanging poised at her side, legs crossed at the knees. With one foot suspended in air and multicolored drapery sweeping rhythmically over her body, she seems vibrant and alive. She does not yet seem to have been illuminated, however, as she still thumbs the pages of a book on her lectern, and her genius only now lights the lamp of revelation. *Act Two*: Isaiah sits facing forward with ankles crossed and drawn back, marking a place in a book with his fingers. His figure is more closed, monochromatic, and inactive than Erythræa. But he has just finished consulting his book, and mental understanding seems at the point of dawning—signaled by his head turning to the light, his left hand beginning to unfold into an upward point. His genius also indicates the light of divine truth by his extended arm and pointing finger, his gesture underscored by the trail of green drapery snaking heavenward like a growing vine.

Joel (Plate 27) was prophet of the outpouring of God's spirit on humanity (Joel 3: 1–2). In Acts 2:17–21 this was interpreted as foretelling the gift of the Holy Spirit at Pentecost when the church received its divine charge to preach the message of Christ to all nations. He also prophesied an apocalyptic time of troubles for the sins of the Israelites,

PLATE 24 - *Cumæan Sibyl*

PLATE 25 - *Erythræan Sibyl*

PLATE 26 - *Isaiah*

PLATE 27 - *Joel*

PLATE 28 - *Delphic Sibyl*

the coming of a "teacher of justice" (Joel 2:23), and a renewed vine. Together, these prophecies symbolized the Last Judgment, the coming of Christ, and the Eucharist. His location near the fallen Noah planting the vine in the *Drunkenness of Noah* is thus apt.

The *Delphic Sibyl* (Plate 28), opposite *Joel*, was a prophetess of virgin birth and an oracle of Apollo. As a seer of a savior coming to redeem Noah's sin, she equally appropriately flanks the *Drunkenness of Noah*.

Joel, enveloped within a rose cape, sits frontally, leaning on a lectern and reading his prophecies on a scroll with quiet concentration. His intellect's intensity is suggested by his contrapposto's vigor. One leg and the opposite shoulder are forward, the other leg and opposite shoulder are drawn back; his head turns contrary to the rotation of his shoulders, his torso inclines diagonally; his limbs in relationship to the spiraling axis of his spine suggest a slow-turning whirligig. The two genii further animate the scene. The one in shadow mirrors Joel's posture and action of reading, while the other, holding a book, points to the first and engages him in discussion.

The Delphic Sibyl (Delphica) has a similar silhouette—an inclined oval—and seated contrapposto. Her left arm and right leg are forward, right arm and left leg withdrawn; her head turns opposite to the rotation of her diagonal-leaning torso. But her body is in three-quarter profile, not frontal, and she looks away from the altar, not toward it. The genii, both with shadowed faces, consult and question a text, and Delphica turns from the light. She seems not yet to have received divine revelation. Her lips are parted, however, as if about to speak, and she prepares to pivot her torso to the right, unroll the scroll across her lap, and grasp the end with her right hand. She will complete her implied rotation ready to read the now-revealed prophecy in a position almost identical to Joel's.

THE MEDALLIONS

*T*en pseudobronze medallions depict Old Testament scenes *sub lege* in parallel with the Moses scenes on the walls below, although the paint has now completely flaked off one of the medallions. All these scenes were derived from woodcuts in the 1493 edition of Niccolò Malermi's popular Italian Bible of which six further editions appeared before 1508. The full texts of these episodes, therefore, were well known to Michelangelo and his intended audience. The *Ascension of Elijah* (2 Kings 2:1–15) (Plate 29a) and

Abraham's Sacrifice of Isaac (Genesis 22:1–18) (Plate 29b) flank the *Separation of Light and Dark*. When Elijah ascended to heaven in a chariot by an act of God, his cloak fell to earth and was put on by Elisha. The transfer of the cloak—illustrated in the woodcut in Malermi's Bible and perhaps also originally in the damaged fresco—was a visible sign of the continuity of divine authority. Since Elisha for Giles of Viterbo was a prototype for Saint Peter and Julius II, the medallion, like the succession of popes on the walls below, was

probably understood as a type of Petrine Succession through which the power of the keys was passed from one pope to the next.

Abraham, who unhesitatingly prepared to sacrifice his own son according to divine command, exemplifies absolute obedience to, and trust in, God's authority.

Isaac, an innocent victim, was a traditional prefiguration of the sacrificial Christ and thus relates to the brooding of Jeremiah and the dark side of the *Separation of Light and Dark*. Similarly, Elijah's ascent alludes to Christ's Ascension, reinforcing the significance of the light side of the *Separation of Light and Dark* and the radiance of the Libyan Sibyl.

The medallion to the left of the *Separation of Water from Firmament* is blank (Plate 29c), but it may originally have represented *Elisha Cures Naaman of Leprosy* (2 Kings 5). If so, it would have underscored God's gift of salvific power to Elisha and linked to the baptismal significance of the *Separation of Water from Firmament*, for Naaman, a ninth-century B.C. commander of the army of the king of Syria, was cured by washing seven times in the Jordan.

The damaged *Death of Absalom* (2 Samuel 18), opposite, shows David's son, Absalom, who unsuccessfully tried to usurp his father's authority (Plate 29d). As he fled David's avenging forces on a

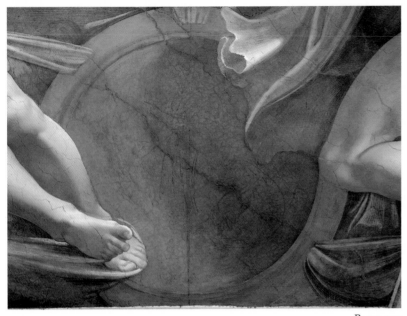

mule, he became entangled in an oak branch. The medallion depicts Absalom dangling in the air by his hair; David's commander, Joab, approaches from the left on a rearing horse ready to kill Absalom with a lance. With David a traditional Christ-type and the oak (in Italian *rovere*) the personal emblem of Julius II (Giuliano della Rovere), the scene was probably understood as rebellion against the church and its leadership and thus properly links with Persica and Daniel, seers of a time of troubles. At the same time, the scene could intimate Christ's redemptive Sacrifice, for traditionally the oak provided both the material of Christ's Cross and acorns, the food of the Golden Age or

Paradise. Reference to Christ's Sacrifice, which made baptism effective, associates the medallion with the *Separation of Water from Firmament*.

The *Death of Nicanor* (2 Maccabees 15) (Plate 29e) and *Alexander the Great before the High Priest of Jerusalem* (Plate 29f) bound the *Creation of Eve*. Nicanor, out to exterminate the Israelites, attacked Jerusalem on the Sabbath, after having raised his hand in a blasphemous oath against the Temple. His forces are shown being defeated by Judas Maccabeus, above whom, from a tower window, hang the head and hands of Nicanor, which Judas Maccabeus had ordered

cut off as punishment for the blasphemous oath. As a symbolic depiction of the fate of those who might launch an attack against the church's spiritual sovereignty, the medallion is particularly apt above Ezekiel, prophet of the purified Temple.

In a scene not written about in the Bible but interpolated in the Malermi Bible at 2 Maccabees 1, the medallion opposite shows the moment when Alexander the Great, having planned to destroy Jerusalem as part of his eastern expansion, was met outside the city by the high priest. So awed was Alexander by the priest that he spared Jerusalem and knelt in prayer to adore the name of God, which had

been worked into the priest's vestments. The priest, in turn, would later tell Alexander that, according to Daniel's prophecy of the four world monarchies (Daniel 2:31–45), his eastern campaign would succeed and that he would establish a Macedonian empire. The high priest's costume and headdress so resemble those of the pope's pontificals and tiara, or temporal crown, that the episode not only suggests that the pope's power is superior to the power of secular sovereigns but that attacks on the church's leadership and sovereignty will be overcome by divine intervention. The fourth world monarchy of Daniel's prophecy, after Alexander's third, was understood to be the Roman Empire into

father of Judas Maccabeus, was a Jew steadfast in his faith and so refused the order of Antiochus Epiphanes, king of Syria, to worship false gods. To dramatize the point, as shown in the medallion, he destroyed in Modein an altar with its idol. Then, as not shown, he killed a Jew, who "in the sight of all" sacrificed to the idols "on the altar…according to the king's order," as well as the messenger of the king "who was forcing them to sacrifice" (1 Maccabees 2:23–25). This episode, then, not only implies an assault on the church's spiritual authority but also foretells the distinction between the acceptable sacrifice of the New Dispensation and unacceptable sacrifices of the Old as also foretold in the *Sacrifice of Noah.*

The *Expulsion of Heliodorus,* opposite, depicts a challenge to the material possessions of the church: Heliodorus, chancellor of Seleucus IV, king of Syria, was sent to Jerusalem to despoil the Temple but was stopped after the high priest Onias called on God for help. As shown in the medallion, there miraculously appeared "a horse, mounted by a dreadful rider. Charging furiously, the horse attacked Heliodorus with its front hoofs…Then two other young men… flogged him unceasingly" (2 Maccabees 3:25–27). Then, as not shown, Onias "offered a sacrifice for the man's recovery," and the same three men who had scourged Heliodorus again miraculously appeared saying: "Be very grateful to the high priest Onias. It is for his sake that the Lord has spared your life" (2 Maccabees 3:31–33). Again, it is the unillustrated end of the narrative that connects the medallion to the *Sacrifice of*

which Christ was born and which marked the beginning of the kingdom that "shall stand forever" (Daniel 2:44). The medallion finds its logical place, therefore, above Cumæa, prophetess of the *pax romana.*

Together in their concern for the pope's supremacy and the church's temporal and spiritual dominion, both medallions considerably expand the meaning of the *Creation of Eve,* symbolic of the church's foundation.

Mattathias Pulls Down the Altar in Modein (1 Maccabees 2) (Plate 29g, page 89) and the *Expulsion of Heliodorus* (2 Maccabees 3) (Plate 29h) are on either side of the *Sacrifice of Noah.* Mattathias,

Noah in which the healing power of an acceptable sacrifice is implicit. In their concern with sacrifices, both medallions relate to the prophecies of Erythræa and Isaiah, which pertain to the Incarnation, Passion, and Resurrection.

Antiochus Epiphanes Falls from His Chariot (2 Maccabees 9) (Plate 29i) and the *Death of Razis* (2 Maccabees 14:37–46) (Plate 29j) are the last pair of medallions flanking the *Drunkenness of Noah*.[5] The first shows Antiochus Epiphanes falling from his chariot on his way to destroy Jerusalem and to exterminate the Jews, such that "he who previously, in his superhuman presumption, thought he could command

the waves of the sea…was now thrown to the ground," bearing witness "to all the power of God" (2 Maccabees 9:8).

On the right side of the opposite medallion, one of the soldiers of a force of more than five hundred sent by Nicanor is shown breaking down the door of Razis's house to arrest him. On the damaged left side, Razis, who was highly regarded and "was called a father of the Jews because of his love for them," prepares to stab himself with his sword, "preferring to die nobly rather than fall into the hands of vile men."

Both medallions feature evil enemies of the Jews and could be, like the cursed Ham in the *Drunkenness of Noah*, signs for Christ's mockers and the church's persecutors. As the innocent victim, Razis could, as does Noah, allude to Christ's Sacrifice. Both scenes are also logically near Joel and Delphica, seers of sinful humanity and a coming savior.

Like the central narratives, the medallions appear to have been planned in responsive and contrasting pairs on either side of the central transverse axis. The *Ascension of Elijah* and *Antiochus Epiphanes Falls from his Chariot* (Plates 29a, 29i) each have a chariot and divine intervention in common, but the first chariot brings salvation through faith, the latter, damnation through a challenge to the faithful. The corresponding pair on the opposite side of the vault, *Abraham's Sacrifice of Isaac* and the *Death of Razis* (Plates 29b, 29j), have in common steadfast religious faith and innocent victims prefiguring the sacrificial Christ. But Abraham, who is obedient to God, is blessed, while Nicanor, who defied God's will by arresting Razis, is killed. Both pairs, then, prefigure the popes' power of the keys to save and to damn.

Elisha Cures Naaman of Leprosy (assuming that this was the missing scene) and *Mattathias Pulls Down the Altar in Modein* (Plates 29c, 29g) share the domination of Palestine by Syrians who attacked Judaism, and two holy Jews who met the Syrian challenge. Both connote the triumph of the spiritual or invisible church. The corresponding pair on the opposite side of the vault, the *Death of Absalom* and the *Expulsion of Heliodorus* (Plates 29d, 29h), depict unsuccessful assaults on the leadership and wealth of Judaism and imply the victory of the institutional church. Elisha cured the enemy; Mattathias killed the enemy's messenger and a heretic Jew. Absalom was slain; Heliodorus was saved. Again, both pairs also indicate the pope's power of the keys.

Whether the scenes are read as pairs on the transverse or the longitudinal axes, one scene in each pair concerns divine intervention, the other, faith, prayer, or active defense of the faith. This implies that both grace and works were necessary for salvation, a doctrine increasingly subject to debate in just these years.

The four medallions above the *sancta sanctorum* (Plates 29a, 29b, 29c, 29d) are from Kings and Samuel, except for *Abraham's Sacrifice of Isaac*, which is from Genesis. The remaining six (Plates 29e, 29f, 29g, 29h, 29i, 29j) come from Malermi's Maccabees. Read from altar to entrance, the medallions on the right side facing the altar are in chronological order (Plates 29b, 29d, 29f, 29h, 29j). Those on the left would also be in chronological order, if the *Death of Nicanor* and the *Antiochus Epiphanes Falls from his Chariot* were interchanged (Plates 29e, 29i). The chronology was probably upset in order for two scenes with chariots to be paired at either end of the longitudinal axis (Plates 29a, 29i) and for Judas Maccabeus to be paired with Alexander the Great and the high priest (Plates 29e, 29f) thus reinforcing, on the all-important central transverse axis, the universal spiritual and temporal sovereignty claimed by Julius.

The *Ignudi*

Mastery of the body, especially the nude, was the essential measure of achievement for any artist in the High Renaissance, especially for a sculptor such as Michelangelo. Nothing offered a greater challenge or source of inspiration to artists in representing the human form than the sculpture of antiquity, which was systematically collected and admired as never before by Julius II and his circle, notwithstanding accusations of paganism by some shocked critics of the Julian regime. The *ignudi* of the Sistine ceiling became a means by which Michelangelo honed his skills at depicting male anatomy, absorbed and then surpassed the examples of classical sculpture, and developed a heroic style analogous to the hyperbole of epideictic rhetoric. They may also have celebrated subliminally his presumed sexual proclivities.

Often overlooked in the triangular spaces above the pendentives and spandrels flanking the rams' skulls (Plates 30, 31) are twenty-four seated and reclining fictive bronze nudes, often with backs turned, who awkwardly twist, kick, and squirm within dark and constricted spaces. Inarticulate and irrational, they exhibit purely animalistic behavior with little self-control. The recent restoration has shown that two of these nudes have the conventional pointed ears of devils (Plate 31). This leaves little doubt that Michelangelo conceived of them as fallen angels who were already prefigured, as we have seen, in the *Separation of Light and Dark*.

Very different in form and meaning are the *ignudi* developed from the winged angels in both of Michelangelo's preliminary sketches for the layout of the ceiling, as we have seen (see figs. 11, 13). Michelangelo has dispensed with the wings, but, in spite of their aggressive masculinity, which has troubled critics to our own day, they are best understood as angels—embodiments of divine spirit and agents of God—who orchestrate and mediate between the earliest history of humankind in the center of the ceiling and the prophecies of the Jews and Gentiles on the sides. Most of the *ignudi* hold ribbons attached to the

PLATE 30 - Fictive bronze nudes between *Ezekiel* and the *Persian Sibyl*

PLATE 31 - Fictive bronze nudes between the *Libyan Sibyl* and *Daniel*

PLATE 32 - *Ignudo* above and to the right of the *Erythræan Sibyl*

PLATE 33 - *Ignudo* above and to the left of *Isaiah*

bronze medallions. They support the representations depicting the operations of divine law within the world *sub lege* and validate their prefigurative significance in the world *sub gratia.* Many of the *ignudi* also hold great swags of green oak leaves with giant golden acorns. Oak garlands were associated in antiquity with Roman emperors and in the Julian period with the pope. As we have seen, oak was also the traditional wood of Christ's Cross and acorns the food of the Golden Age. Thus the *igundi* also seem to uphold papal claims to imperial sovereignty and confirm the promise of regeneration and salvation symbolized throughout the ceiling, including the liberal use of the colors green and gold.

The nudes surrounding the first two bays are variations of a well-known classical type found on medals and carved cameos and gems. An example well known to Michelangelo—*Diomedes and the Palladium,* once in the collection of Lorenzo de' Medici (fig. 28, page 33)—served as a model in reverse for the nude above and to the right of the *Erythæan Sibyl* (Plate 32).

The nude directly opposite, above and to the left of *Isaiah,* who leans aggressively forward into the viewer's space (Plate 33), draws his inspiration from the first-century A.D. *Laocoön* (fig. 29, page 33). Found in Rome in 1506 and displayed in the Vatican sculpture collection of Julius II, this marble group made a profound impact on Renaissance artists, especially on Michelangelo, who restored the work. This is clearly evident from the close relationships in posture, gesture,

and musculature between the *ignudo* and Laocoön. It is also clear that at this stage in his artistic development Michelangelo was still coming to terms with his classical exemplars, not outdoing them.

With the nude near the *Separation of Water from Firmament* from the second campaign (Plate 34), Michelangelo has created nothing less than a whole new figure canon characterized by more developed muscles, narrower hips, broader shoulders, a thicker torso, and a higher center of gravity. Together these new elements communicate greater strength and grace than ever before. The intensity of drama also exceeds even that of the *Laocoön,* a drama expressed by the contrary diagonal axes of torso and limbs, the curled toe, the strongly turned shoulders, the intense expression, and the hair flying forward in response to the figure's almost violent leap backward.

The last bay demonstrates the sheer technical virtuosity of Michelangelo now in full command of the nude (Plate 35). The *ignudo* to the left of God separating light and dark communicates supreme linear grace developed along a diagonal axis by means of a somewhat flattened but relaxed body in a complex contrapposto with an incisive, angular silhouette. By contrast, his companion to the right leans diagonally in the opposite direction within a more closed, curvilinear silhouette. His body is exceptionally massive and thick and every muscle strains and bulges in a tense play of counterbalanced parts. A comparison with the famous *Torso Belvedere* of c. 150 B.C. in the Vatican (fig. 30, page 33) indicates just how far beyond any known work of

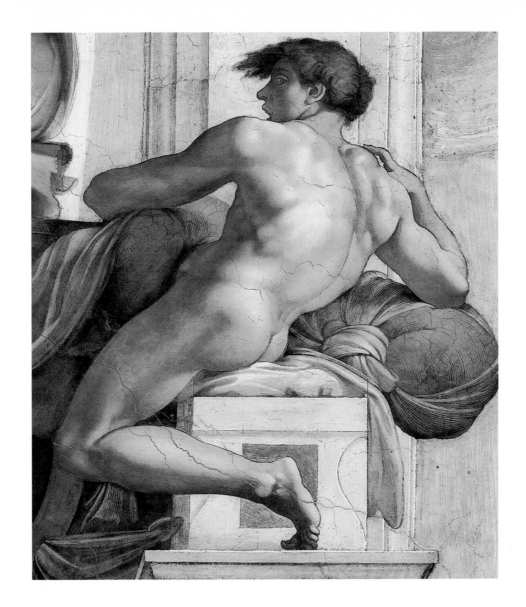

PLATE 34 - *Ignudo*
above and to the right
of the *Persian Sibyl*

PLATE 35 - *Ignudi* to the left of the *Separation of Light and Dark*

PLATE 36 - *Ignudi* to the right of the *Separation of Light and Dark*

classical antiquity Michelangelo had advanced in terms of titanic scale, muscular power, and compressed density. It was impossible to develop further this new heroic canon without breaking the bonds of what is possible or plausible in human anatomy.

Variations within the canon were possible, however, as the two nudes on the opposite side of the bay illustrate (Plate 36). The *ignudo* to the right is constructed around a vertical axis defined by his head and the edge of the cubic seat. His body is contained within an ovoid silhouette that appears hollow at the center. Yet within this rather closed, regular, and stable shape, the nude expresses a huge potential for movement by the strong torsion of diagonally disposed limbs and torso.

His companion is also designed on a vertical axis, but his body is as solid as imaginable at the center and circumscribed by an open, irregular, and active silhouette. In a kind of bilateral contrapposto, contrasting in every respect with the *ignudo* to his left, he stretches out his limbs and torso to the right side of his spine for the highest expression of muscular tension and contracts them on the left side for a maximum of organic compression.

Within the developmental scope of the Sistine ceiling, Michelangelo has in this last bay reached the absolute limits of anatomical variation and perfection, creating nudes that embody more Herculean power and Apollonian refinement than ever before, nudes that are the consummate expressions of angelic grace.

THE ANCESTORS OF CHRIST

The sixteen lunettes and eight spandrels depict the forty generations of males recorded in Matthew 1:1–16 (for example, figs. 31, 32 and Plates 37, 38). They represent Christ's physical lineage from Abraham to Joseph. The papal succession, it was believed, continued Christ's spiritual lineage from Peter to the present. The ancestors, therefore, are logically closest to the series of fifteenth-century popes and organized in a similar manner.

The series of ancestors begins on the west wall to the left of the altar. It had at first continued to the right in two lunettes, but these were destroyed by Michelangelo's *Last Judgment;* nevertheless, these lunettes are known from drawings and prints (figs. 31, 32). The series of ancestors proceeds zigzag down the chapel to the entrance, reading from south (left) to north (right) and back again. There is only one exception: Two consecutive groups of ancestors—those in the lunette inscribed Ezechias, Manasses, and Amon, and those in the lunette inscribed Josias, Jechonias, and Salathiel—are side by side on the north wall rather than on walls opposite each other. This may have been done in order to allow the series to end in the right lunette on the east entrance wall directly opposite where it begins on the west altar wall.

There are ninety-one figures in the lunettes and spandrels,

most without special attributes. This makes it difficult to attach the forty inscribed names to individual figures. With a total of only twenty-eight adult males, the difficulty is compounded, since at least twelve of the thirty-six children must be ancestors.

With the exception of Abraham (fig. 31), every adult male is accompanied by an adult female, unprecedented within the tradition of ancestor representations. The figures in the lunettes are depicted as if indoors, mostly sitting on benches in shallow architectural spaces. The figures in the spandrels are shown as if outdoors, mostly sitting or reclining on shallow foreshortened ledges of barren ground. These spaces are separate from the painted architectural system of the ceiling, seemingly excavated from the thickness of the wall. Illuminated by raking, often nocturnal light, the figures are strongly shadowed and three-dimensional and thus appear to inhabit the actual space of the chapel. Their immediacy is heightened by actions that appear mundane. Many stare silently into space, meditate, or sleep, listlessly awaiting something to happen. Others are more animated with activities "naturally" coded by gender. Men engage in mental pursuits such as reading, writing, observing, and peregrinating (as signaled by walking sticks and dress). Women possess household items—key, purse, scissors, mirror,

Fig. 31 - After Michelangelo, *Abraham, Isaac, Jacob, and Judas* lunette, engraving

Fig. 32 - After Michelangelo, *Phares, Esron, and Aran* lunette, engraving

cradle, spindle, plate, stool, towel, comb—and perform domestic tasks such as grooming, spinning, sewing, or tending children.

The weary waiting or humdrum endeavors of the ancestors cue their limited place within the divine plan of history. They merely pass on the physical seed of Christ with little, if any, spiritual awareness through the Old Testament to the beginning of the New. Moreover, the advanced age of most of the men and two of the women, the absence of much meaningful interaction between the sexes, the sterile settings, and the general atmosphere of lethargy and darkness all suggest impotence and death. With Isaac, who carries the wood for his own sacrifice (fig. 31), impeding death is explicit.

Most of the women and a few men, however, are young and potent. One woman is pregnant, and many others either nurse or embrace children. These children, often quite animated, suggest that most of the pairs of adult men and women are family groups. The light that falls on these groups comes from the direction of the altar, a common indication of divine illumination. Together these signs of fecundity allude to Christ's promise of regeneration.

All of the children among the ancestors appear to be males until the last lunette (Plate 38). Here the series ends presumably with Jacob and Joseph on the left accompanied by the Virgin and the infant Christ on the right, although Michelangelo seems to have been deliberately ambiguous about their identities. The final figure to the right, however, is clearly a female child. She hands the putative Christ Child what looks to be bread. Both her gender and attribute suggest that she is a concluding symbol of the church and its sacrament of salvation.

PLATE 37 - *Asa, Josaphat, and Joran*

Plate 38 - *Jacob and Joseph*

CONCLUSION

Michelangelo has represented an unusually large number of women (and female infants) in the ceiling. In every case they are paired with men (and male infants), thus suggesting the human capacity for physical reproduction. This reproductive potential, in turn, is a major metaphor in the ceiling for spiritual renewal. Within this coupling, Michelangelo has created a hierarchy of human form and action directly related to the degree of participation in, and understanding of, the divine plan. The inarticulate bodies and animalistic movements of the bronze nudes above the spandrels and pendentives signal an absence or rejection of spiritual awareness. The tired indifference and commonplace acts of the ancestors suggest participation in the ceiling's great drama only at the physical, not the spiritual level. The playful lovemaking of the infants supporting the entablature of the thrones implies human innocence uncorrupted by sin before the Fall. Their youth, diminutive size, and limited roles, however, indicate that they act with little knowledge. Michelangelo cues the foreknowledge, if not complete revelation, of the prophets and sibyls by their size, strength, and acts of contemplation, discussion, reading, and writing. The *ignudi* are images of divine perfection, as we have seen, but their relatively trivial deeds of supporting the medallions mark their status as mere agents of God's will. At the top of the hierarchy is Adam. Like the *ignudi*, he is endowed with the beauty, grace, youth, and strength of divinity, but unlike them, he has also been given the godlike freedom to act independently.

This scheme of humankind's willed ascent toward spiritual understanding expressed by ever-greater external beauty and autonomy was particularly fitting for a sculptor, as Michelangelo always considered himself to be, whose means of communication were largely limited to the body and its movements. The notion was also fully consistent with one of the major philosophical currents of the High Renaissance, Neoplatonism, a philosophy that Michelangelo learned when living in the household of Lorenzo de' Medici from 1490 to 1492 and which he references repeatedly in his poetry. In addition, rhetorical praise for the human potential to achieve by force of will a dignity consonant with the perfection of God, especially as formulated by the Florentine Neoplatonist Pico della Mirandola (1463–94), was a much repeated theme in sermons preached to the *capella papalis* in the years around the execution of the ceiling.

The Sistine ceiling, in conclusion, can be characterized as Christological and Incarnational—fallen and sinful humankind depended on the coming of Christ; soteriological and Neoplatonic—humankind was atoned, elevated, and saved by Christ's Sacrifice; ecclesiological and papal—the institution of the church with its priestly hierarchy headed by a pope, who claimed universal spiritual and temporal power, was the necessary channel of God's redemptive grace; sacramental and penitential—the ritual means for channeling the potential for salvation were baptism and the Eucharist, requiring both divine grace and personal faith, prayer, and sacrifice; and teleological and eschatological—history was preordained from the beginning, unfolded according to God's plan through time *ante legem, sub lege,* and *sub gratia* with pre-Christian prefiguring Christian history, and culminated in both a millennial time of troubles and Golden Age at the end of time.

These complex, multileveled, and overlapping denotative and connotative levels of the program, most aspects of which were either strongly affirmed or denied in the Julian era, are held in tense equilibrium by Michelangelo's interlocking linear, diadic, and triadic narrative organization, responsive and contrasting compositional structure, and hierarchy of anatomical form and action. The entire ensemble is given archetypal conviction and cosmic force by Michelangelo's heroic style grounded in the naturalism and classical revival of the Renaissance.

Notes to the Commentaries

[1] Avraham Ronen, "An Antique Prototype for Michelangelo's Fall of Man," *Journal of the Warburg and Courtauld Institutes* 37 (1974): 356–58.

[2] The son leading the ram and the wife receiving the entrails were repainted by Domenico Carnevali in c. 1568, which accounts for their awkwardness.

[3] For sibyls, see Creighton E. Gilbert, "The Proportion of Women," *Michelangelo, On and Off the Sistine Ceiling. Selected Essays* (New York, 1994), 58–113; Gail L. Geiger, *Filippino Lippi's Carafa Chapel* (Kirksville, Mo., 1986), 55–72.

[4] For Christ as Apollo in the Vatican, see Elisabeth Schröter, "Der Vatikan als Hügel Apollons und der Musen. Kunst und Panegyrik von Nikolaus V. bis Julius II.," *Römische Quartalschrift* 75 (1980): 208–40.

[5] Rab Hatfield, "Trust in God: The Sources of Michelangelo's Frescoes on the Sistine Ceiling," *Occasional Papers Published by Syracuse University*, Florence, Italy 1 (1990): 2, is the first to correctly identify the Death of Razis. When the missing part of the medallion (lost along with most of the flanking *ignudo* as a result of the 1797 explosion in the Castel Sant'Angelo) is reconstructed with the aid of an engraving by Cherubino Alberti (see Alida Moltedo, *La Sistina Riprodotta. Gli affreschi di Michelangelo dalle stampe del Cinquecento alle campagne fotografiche Anderson* [Rome, 1991], 114, fig. 27/3), it is clear that the scene is closer to the 1493 Malermi illustration of the death of Razis than to Joab's killing Abner (2 Samuel 3), the usual identification of the scene. Furthermore, since all the other medallions above the eastern half of the chapel are from the two books of Maccabees, it is logical to assume that this one would be, too.

GLOSSARY

AFFRESCO (from the word for "fresh"; in English, "fresco"). Painting on freshly laid plaster with pigments dissolved in water. As plaster and paint dry together, they become united chemically. Known as "true" fresco (or "buon fresco"), but frequently used in combination with "secco" (see below) details, this technique was in general use for mural painting in Italy from the late thirteenth century on.

ARRICCIO (literally, "rough"). The first layer of plaster (and sometime pozzolana, powdered volcanic rock) spread on the masonry in preparation for painting; the "sinopia" (see below) is executed on this surface. It was purposely left rough so that the top layer (see "intonaco") would adhere to it more firmly.

CARTONE (from the word for "heavy paper"; in English "cartoon"). An enlarged version of the main lines of the final composition done on paper or cloth, sometimes, but not always, equal in size to the area to be painted. The cartoon was used to transfer the design to the wall; it could be divided into several sections for the creation of one large image. The cartoon was laid against the wall over the final layer of fresh plaster, so that outlines of the forms could be either incised with a stylus or transferred by "pouncing" (see "spolvero"). In either case, the outlines were used as guides for the artist to paint. The procedure was in common use by the second half of the fifteenth century although it had been developed earlier.

GIORNATA (from the word for "day"). The patch of "intonaco" to be painted "daily," not necessarily in one day. The artist decided in advance the size of the surface he would paint and laid on top of the "arriccio" or rough plaster only the amount of fresh "intonaco" or fine plaster needed for his work. The joinings usually are discernible upon a close examination of the painted surface, and they disclose the order in which the patches were painted because each successive patch slightly overlaps the preceding one.

INTONACO (literally "whitewash," or fine plaster). The final smooth layer of plaster on which painting with colors was carried out. Made from lime, fine sand, and marble dust and laid in sections (see "giornata").

POUNCE, POUNCING Fine powder, ususally pulverized charcoal, dusted over a stencil to transfer a design to an underlying surface.

SECCO (literally "dry"). Painting on plaster that has already dried. The colors are mixed with an adhesive or binder to attach the color to the surface to be painted. The binding medium may be made from various substances, such as tempera. "Tempera" (pigment and animal or vegetable glue) or less often "tempera grassa" (pigment and egg) was commonly used to complete a composition already painted in fresco. Because the pigment and the dry wall surface do not become thoroughly united, as they do in true fresco, mural paintings done in tempera (or "a secco") tend to deteriorate and flake off the walls more rapidly.

SINOPIA Originally a red ochre named after Sinope, a town on the Black Sea that was well known for its red pigments. In fresco technique the term was used for the final preparatory drawing on the "arriccio," which was normally executed in red ochre.

SPOLVERO (from the word for "dust"). An early method (see "cartone") of transferring the artist's drawings onto the "intonaco." After drawings as large as the frescoes were made on paper, their outlines were pricked, and the paper was cut into pieces the size of each day's work. After the day's patch of "intonaco" was laid, the corresponding drawing was placed over it and "dusted" with a cloth sack filled with charcoal powder, some of which passed through the tiny punctured holes to mark the design on the fresh "intonaco."

Selected Bibliography

Ackerman, James S. *The Architecture of Michelangelo*. London, 1961.

Barolsky, Paul. *Michelangelo's Nose. A Myth and Its Maker*. University Park and London, 1990.

Burke, Peter. *Culture and Society in Renaissance Italy, 1420–1540*. New York, 1972.

Condivi, Ascanio. *The Life of Michelangelo*. Trans. Alice Sedgwick Wohl. Ed. Hellmut Wohl. Baton Rouge, 1976.

Dotson, Esther Gordon. "An Augustinian Interpretation of Michel-angelo's Sistine Ceiling." *Art Bulletin* 61 (1979): 223–56, 405–29.

Einem, Herbert von. *Michelangelo*. Trans. Ronald Taylor. London, 1959.

Emison, Patricia. "Michelangelo's Adam, Before and After Creation." *Gazette des Beaux-Arts* 112 (1988): 115–18.

Ettlinger, L. D. *The Sistine Chapel before Michelangelo. Religious Imagery and Papal Primacy*. Oxford, 1965.

Freedberg, Sydney J., *Painting of the High Renaissance in Rome and Florence*, 2 vols. Cambridge, Mass., 1961.

Gilbert, Creighton E. *Michelangelo, On and Off the Sistine Ceiling. Selected Essays*. New York, 1994.

Hartt, Frederick. "'Lignum vitae in medio paradisi.' The Stanza d'Eliodoro and the Sistine Ceiling." *Art Bulletin* 32 (1950): 115–45, 181–218.

———. *The Drawings of Michelangelo*. London, 1971.

Hibbard, Howard. *Michelangelo*. New York, 1974.

Hirst, Michael. *Michelangelo and His Drawings*. New Haven and London, 1988.

Hope, Charles. "The Medallions on the Sistine Ceiling." *Journal of the Warburg and Courtauld Institutes* 50 (1987): 200–04.

Lewine, Carol F. *The Sistine Chapel Walls and the Roman Liturgy*. University Park and London, 1993.

Mancinelli, Fabrizio, and Anna Maria De Strobel. *Michelangelo. Le lunette e le vele della Cappella Sistina, Liber Generationis Jesu Christi*. Rome, 1992.

Michelangelo e la Sistina. La tecnica, il restauro, il mito. Exhibition catalog. Fondazione Giorgio Cini, Venice. Rome, 1990.

Moltedo, Alida, et al. *La Sistina Riprodotta. Gli affreschi di Michelagelo dalle stampe del Cinquecento alle campagne fotografiche Anderson*. Exhibition catalog. Istituto Nazionale per la Grafica. Rome, 1991.

O'Malley, John. *Giles of Viterbo on Church and Reform. A Study in Renaissance Thought*. Leiden, 1968.

———. *Praise and Blame in Renaissance Rome. Rhetoric, Doctrine and Reform in the Sacred Orators of the Papal Court, c. 1450–1521*. Duke Monographs in Medieval and Renaissance Studies, Vol. 5. Durham, N.C., 1979.

Partridge, Loren. *The Art of Renaissance Rome, 1400–1600*. New York and London, 1996.

Partridge, Loren, and Randolph Starn. *A Renaissance Likeness. Art and Culture in Raphael's "Julius II."* Berkeley and Los Angeles, 1980.

Pietrangeli, Carlo, et al. *The Sistine Chapel. The Art, the History, and the Restoration*. New York, 1986.

Ramsden, E.H., ed. *The Letters of Michelangelo*. 2 vols. Stanford, Calif., 1963.

Reeves, Marjorie, ed. *Prophetic Rome in the High Renaissance Period*. Oxford, 1992.

Ronen, Avraham. "An Antique Prototype for Michelangelo's Fall of Man." *Journal of the Warburg and Courtauld Institutes* 37 (1974): 356–58.

Sandström, Sven. "The Sistine Chapel Ceiling." In *Levels of Unreality. Studies in Structure and Construction in Italian Mural Painting During the Renaissance*, 173–91. Uppsala, 1963.

Saslow, James M. *The Poetry of Michelangelo*. New Haven and London, 1991.

Seymour, Charles, Jr., ed. *Michelangelo. The Sistine Chapel Ceiling*. New York, 1972.

Shearman, John. *Raphael's Cartoons in the Collection of Her Majesty the Queen and the Tapestries for the Sistine Chapel*. London, 1972.

Sinding-Larsen, Staale. "A Re-Reading of the Sistine Ceiling." *Acta ad Archaeologiam et Artium Historiam Pertinentia* 4 (1969): 143–57.

Steinberg, Leo. "Who's Who in Michelangelo's Creation of Adam: A Chronology of the Picture's Reluctant Self-Revelation." *Art Bulletin* 74 (1992): 552–66.

Steinmann, Ernst. *Die Sixtinische Kapelle*. 3 vols. Munich, 1901 and 1905.

Stinger, Charles L. *The Renaissance in Rome*. Bloomington, Ind., 1985.

Tolnay, Charles de. *Michelangelo*. 5 vols. Princeton, N.J., 1943–60.

———. *Corpus dei disegni di Michelangelo*. 4 vols. Novara, 1971–80.

Vasari, Giorgio. *La Vita di Michelangelo nelle redazioni del 1550 e del 1568*. 5 vols. Ed. Paola Barocchi. Milan and Naples, 1962.

Wallace, William E. "Michelangelo's Assistants in the Sistine Chapel." *Gazette des Beaux-Arts*, ser. 6, vol. 110 (1987): 203–16.

Warnke, Martin. *The Court Artist. On the Ancestry of the Modern Artist*. Trans. David McLintock. Cambridge, 1993.

Wind, Edgar. "The Ark of Noah: A Study in the Symbolism of Michelangelo." *Measure* 1 (1950): 411–21.

Wittkower, Rudolph and Margot Wittkower. *Born under Saturn. The Character and Conduct of Artists*. London, 1963.

List of Figures

List of Color Plates

Plate 1 (p. 40-41): Michelangelo, Sistine Chapel ceiling, Vatican, 1508–12

Central Narratives

Plate 2 (p. 43): *Separation of Light and Dark*

Plate 3 (p. 44-45): *Creation of Sun, Moon, and Plants*

Plate 4 (p. 47): *Separation of Water from Firmament and Water Brings Forth Life*

Plate 5 (p. 48-49): *Creation of Adam*

Plate 6 (p. 51): *Creation of Eve*

Plate 7 (p. 53): *Temptation and Expulsion*

Plate 8 (p. 55): *Sacrifice of Noah*

Plate 9 (p. 57): *Flood*

Plate 10 (p. 59): *Flood* (detail)

Plate 11 (p. 59): *Flood* (detail)

Plate 12 (p. 61): *Drunkenness of Noah*

Pendentives

Plate 13 (p. 64): *David and Goliath*

Plate 14 (p. 65): *Judith and Holofernes*

Plate 15 (p. 67): *Brazen Serpent*

Plate 16 (p. 69): *Death of Haman*

Prophets and Sibyls

Plate 17 (p. 72): *Zechariah*

Plate 18 (p. 73): *Jonah*

Plate 19 (p. 76): *Jeremiah*

Plate 20 (p. 77): *Libyan Sibyl*

Plate 21 (p. 78): *Persian Sibyl*

Plate 22 (p. 79): *Daniel*

Plate 23 (p. 81): *Ezekiel*

Plate 24 (p. 83): *Cumæan Sibyl*

Plate 25 (p. 84): *Erythræan Sibyl*

Plate 26 (p. 85): *Isaiah*

Plate 27 (p. 86): *Joel*

Plate 28 (p. 87): *Delphic Sibyl*

DATE DU

HIGHSMITI